A JOURNEY TO REMEMBER ...AND OTHER MUSINGS

ONE PHOTOGRAPHER'S VIEW OF THE PRESENT, TO REVEAL THE PAST

BY
PAUL E. DONIHUE

Solid Ground Publications

Solid Ground Publications
2708 Cleveland Rd, Ste 200
Wooster, Oh 44691

What Others Are Saying About "A Journey To Rember ...And Other Musings"

"As I read this book and realized what the author had gone thru to capture these pictures, I could see through his eyes, a different meaning to old. The pictures are great, but the printed word in this book is outstanding. Made me want to know the background behind each picture, and why each thing was abandoned, besides age. ...The photographs are beautifully done. They have heart." - Elly Brenner, Texas

"I loved it, however; when I got to the end...I wanted to see more. I keep trying to get my mouse to scroll forward, but it would not let me." -Pastor Larry Murphy, Ohio

"The book inspired thought & feelings. It was very nice. They (the photographs) were great, very well done. " Jason Felts, CEO, Florida

"Very impressed with the preview, cant wait to see the rest of the book. Old things have a way of getting to me. I'm always mesmerized by them and find myself wondering what their story is. And when I have their stories I'm in 7th heaven. ...Hurry with the book so I can finish reading it." -Stephanie Loeppky, Louisiana

Table of Contents

My Tribute and Dedication:

This photography book is dedicated to several very important people in my life. It is not always easy to follow and love an entrepreneurial person. My wife, Pat, of nearly forty-five years has been my rock and support system through twenty-three years of ministry; ten years as a sales-person, manager and regional manager for a private cemetery-funeral home company; eight years owning my own businesses; as well as being an author, consultant, developer of turn-key business systems, seminar speaker, husband, father and grandfather. Through it all, she has been there for me. She is the love of my life. She has believed in me even during difficult times.

To my sons and my daughter-in-laws, Bryan (Chris) and Jeffrey (Jennifer) who have always challenged me to be better at whatever I do, whether in business or as their father. They are very different from each other and yet each of them bring me a breath of fresh air on their outlooks on life, business, parenting, grand-parenting, and of course, photography. They believe in my photography.

And finally, but very important to me, are all seven of my grand-children. Each and every one is unique, gifted, caring, forgiving, and indeed, "just wonderful." Theirs is an unconditional love. I am proud of them and proud to be their grandfather.

In some small way, hopefully the message and photographs in this book will inspire each of them to value the past, embrace the present, and dream big dreams for the future.

Acknowledgements

There are indeed a host of people who have believed in my photography and encouraged me along the way. To each of them, friend and/or client, I am eternally grateful. Three people have contributed greatly to this book.

My dear friend of twenty-eight years, Benjamin (Doug) Baith, has helped me immensely with this project. He has chauffeured me to incredible places and people he has known whereby I could use my photographer's eye and capture the moment in time. He has searched out and suggested places, people, and things that would allow me to complete this task. Most of all, I so appreciate his support and belief in me, not only as a pastor, businessman, and professional photographer, but as "friend."

My oldest son, Bryan, (also my partner in our national business solutions company,) is a graphic artist by training and a very good one. His support and help in suggesting design ideas for this book is worth more than money could pay. Above his expert advise is his belief in my photography and his assistance in helping me to become much better with the software that helps a photographer so much. I owe him so much.

I could not have photographed, or even found some of the items in this book, without the help of Ron Taylor, owner of Third Door Antiques, Wooster, Oh. I had been in Ron's store several times without really realizing the wealth of incredible items of historic value that he has. He has been so kind as to allow me to photograph many of his items for this book. But even more than that, what wonderful fun I had discovering these treasures, and hearing their stories. Some, I had never seen or known about before, and some brought back long forgotten memories. All, I would have missed had I not met Ron and his wonderful wife, Tamala, a couple of years back

Some Thoughts...

This is a book about endings. Whether it is a building, a car or truck, a pedal car or any other item, they most often start useful and beautiful. Somewhere along the line we have become a throw-away society. If we do not need it any longer, it stops working, or a myriad of other reasons, we just hoard it, throw it away, stop using it, put it in the back pasture, let it rust and decay. Many times if it is large enough, it becomes a catch-all for all the other stuff being "collected."

Two events started me off on this journey of remembering and honoring the past. One was that I became completely immersed and dedicated to the art and craft of photography. I learned to see at all times as if I was looking through a viewfinder or LCD screen. Professional photographers see things that many others do not see.

And then, I saw a wonderful photograph of an old, old bus, taken by a member of the Cleveland Photographic Society. I was mesmerized by the photo and my bucket list of photography images began with the desire to find the "perfect" old truck, by which I could make a gorgeous photograph.

Since that time, I have been captivated by and on mission to record photographically broken down things, primarily buildings and vehicles, among others. Once proud, useful, and important to society. Now discarded, rusting and decaying away, not to be actively used again.

Noteworthy is the fact that there is a lot of interest these days in the old "rust buckets" of things that could be destined for the junk pile, if not rescued by some kindred spirit. We baby boomers, and others, are "remembering" past times and showing an interest in collecting, sometimes restoring, and often just remembering those items of the past that was involved in our society, oh, so many years ago.

I want you to know that these items can be incredibly beautiful in photographic images. ...And that is what this book is all about. I have traveled dozens, hundreds and even thousands of miles to find these incredible shots. So let's go on a trip together. One that will lead us from the past right to the present on an incredible photographic journey.

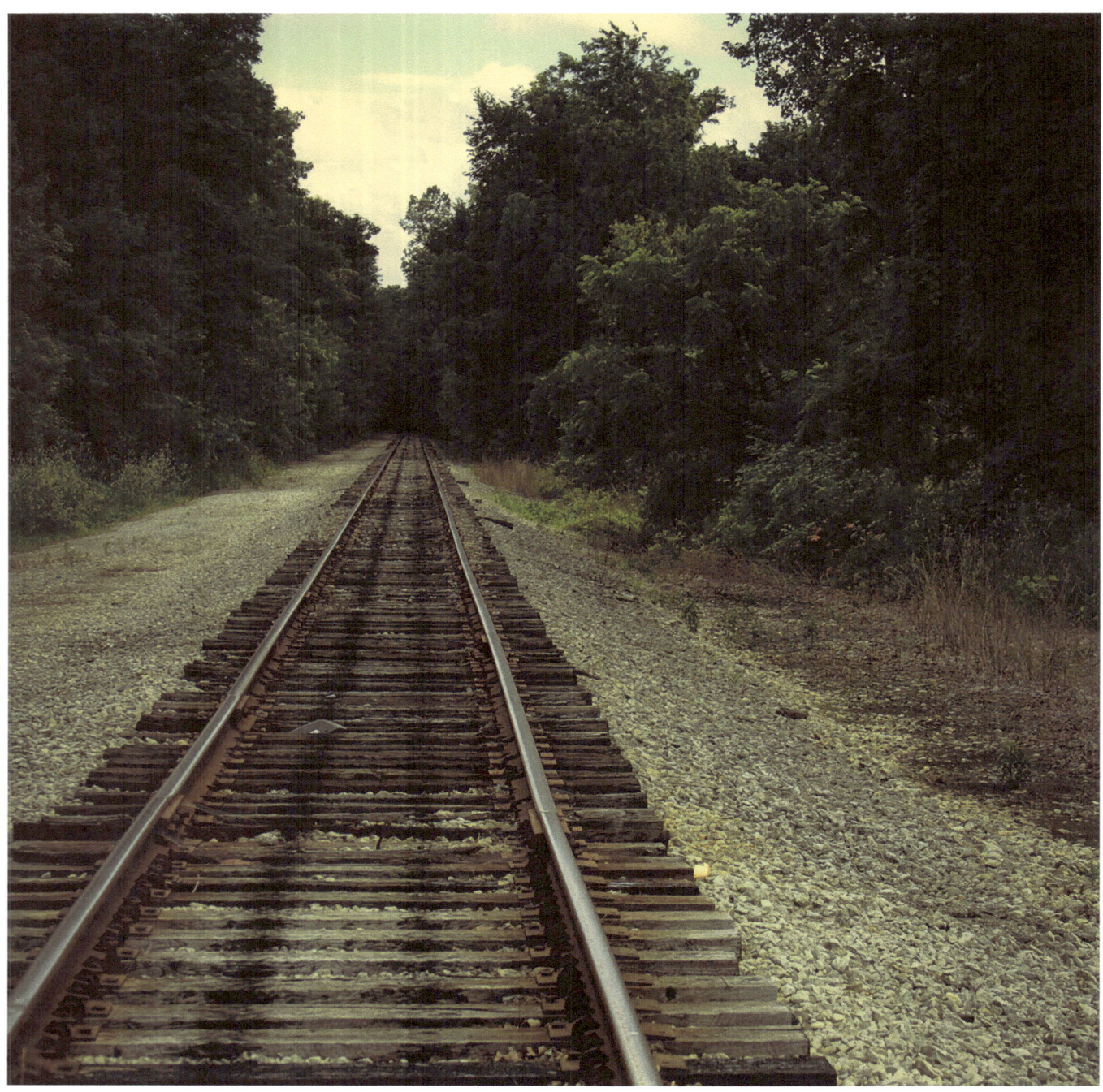

A Journey To Remember

Join me on this wonderful journey. It will bring back memories and at the same time tell you how I came to see some of these incredible things and places. If you are young enough not to have remembered these things even existed, may I say to you that you have missed an incredible time in our lives. Savor this journey. Please don't dismiss it.

Take your time. The train does not move fast. Study the images. There are hidden treasures in each one. That is part of the fun of the journey. If you just glance at them you will never experience all that you can, and again, you will have missed out.

May I suggest not to mourn the past but to embrace today, being aware of the journey many have taken to get to where we are.

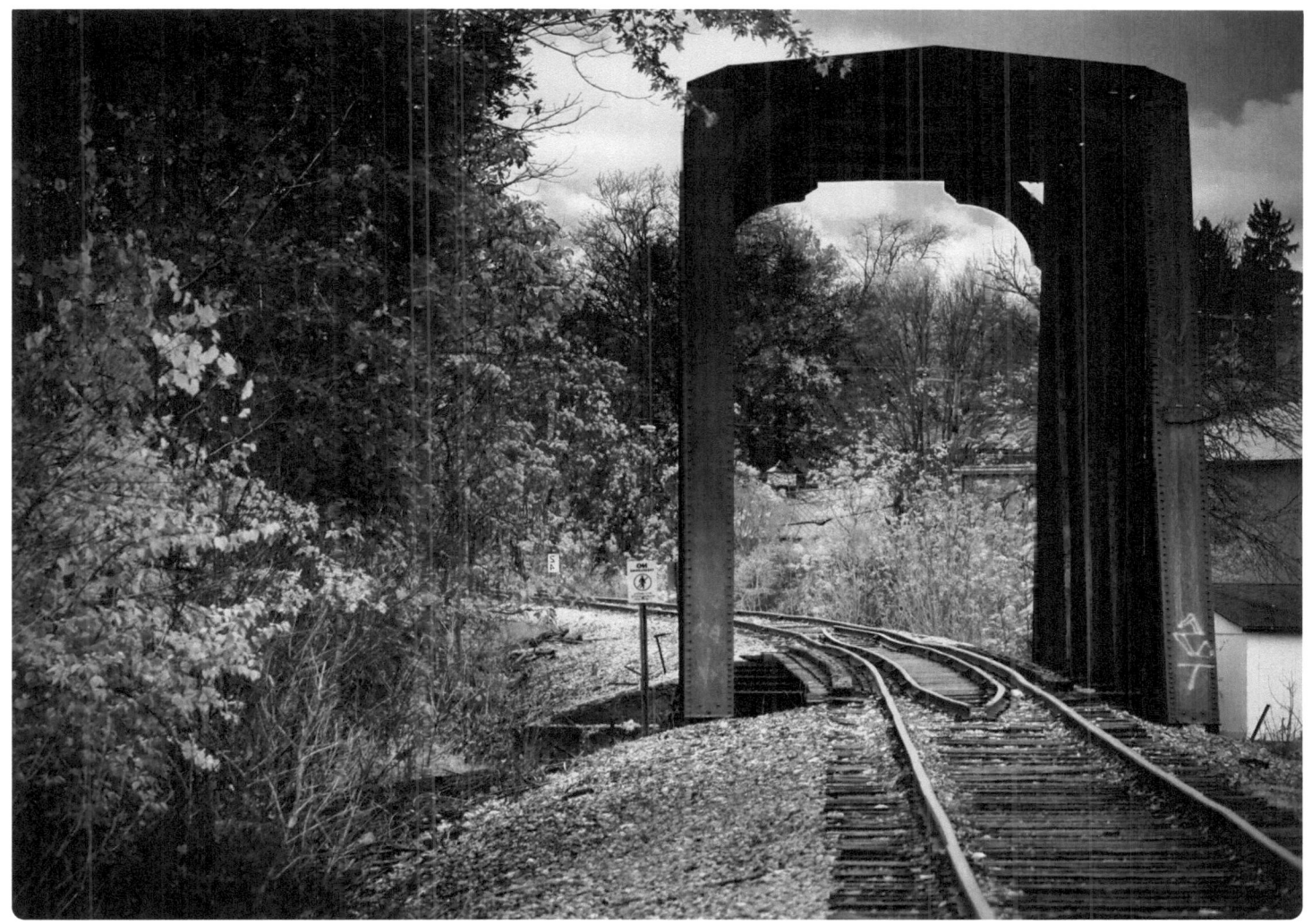

My cameras and gear are not often too far away when I am on a trip, be it pleasure or business. I had just finished my meeting and was looking around when I saw this railroad track and its bridge. What struck me was that the tracks just seemed to disappear into the background, or may I suggest, "the past."

From the present to the past. These photos are like that. They are here today, in the present, showing all kinds of things as they are, and the past has just faded away.

The items and buildings in this book are tired, worn out, no longer kept up, rusted, abandoned and ready for the scrap heap. They are discards, often times there, but likely paid little, if any, attention to anymore. They are left to decay, to fall apart, to quit working and running. They are misfits in a world that is passing them by.

The photography on these pages has been taken because there are still some of us who notice, whose attention is grabbed, who is mesmerized by what has happened to those once vital items of the past. We remember those items and buildings with fondness, now that they are part of our past. It is my hope that they will help you to do that as well.

The photographs are not meant to disturb but are there to remind us that the world continues to change, and that even though we are so quick to embrace the present and the future, we need to at least stop, ponder and remember where we have come from.

That bridge is like a connection from the present to the past. Railroad tracks are a good way to remind us to take a journey. One that brings us to reflect more, to remember more, to be thankful more, to admire more, not just the bright and beautiful, but the things that have paved the way for us today.

And, so, ... the pages and photographs of this book take you on a journey to the broken, the discarded, the forgotten. One that has to be, but a journey nonetheless.

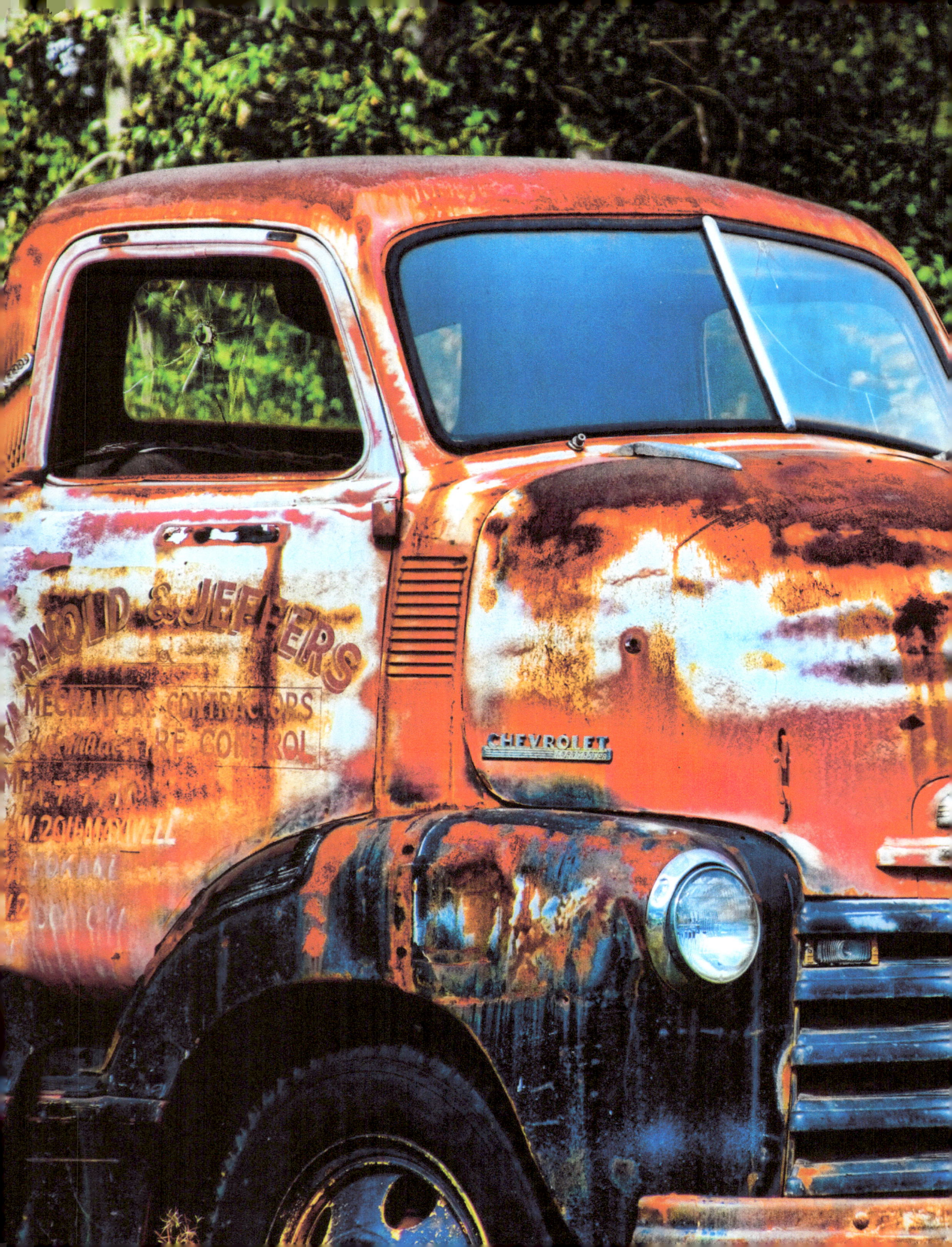

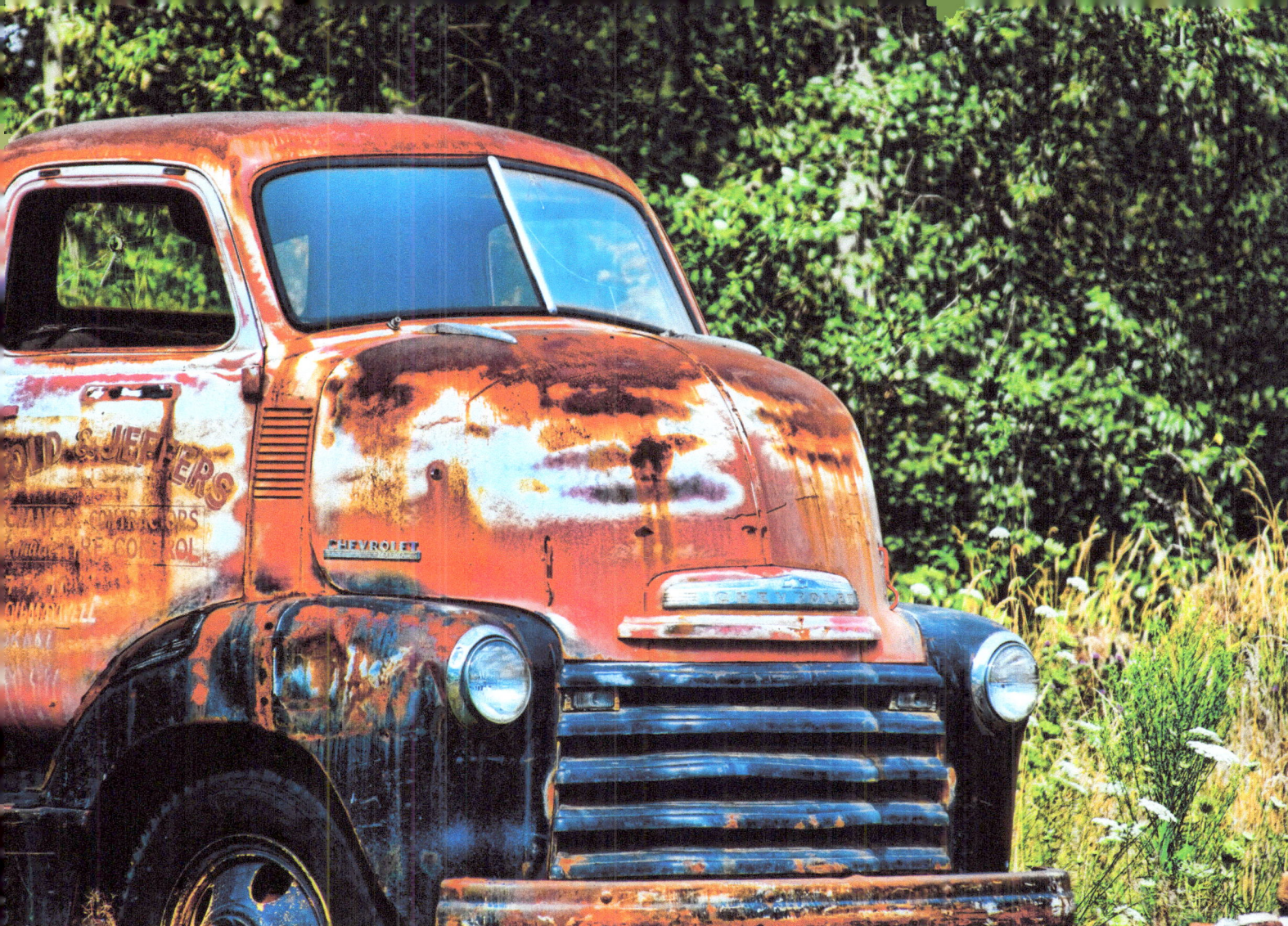

She Found It In About Ten Minutes

I had been seeking out a special old truck for two years. A truck that would signify that my quest to find that cool, old, rusty, mighty truck, had been successful. It had to be a truck with character, with history, with flair, and colorful to boot. My quest had taken me many miles. I had looked intentionally in the back roads of South Carolina, and in the rolling hills of Ohio. But to no avail. Now, on vacation, I found myself going towards Mt. Rainier National Forest, in the beautiful state of Washington.

My sister-in-law was riding in the front seat with me as she, my brother, and I, headed on a sight-seeing trek bound for Mt. Rainier and its National Park that Sunday. I shared with her my search and asked that she keep her "eye out" for this hidden treasure I was looking for. I really did not expect much to happen. Boy, would I be surprised!

Incredibly, within minutes, she said, "There's one," as I passed it going rather fast. Then a minute or two later, "There's one," and again, this time giving me a little warning, she indicated, "there's one." Yes, I had searched for nearly two years, and here, within ten minutes she had found three! I was incredulous, but excited as I turned the car around and drove trepidly into the driveway of this house/business.

And there it was, this gorgeous, rusty, well used, Chevy truck. Colorful, distinct, with a stately aura about it. It even had the name of the company on the doors. I could not wait to get back to my brother's home to see fully what my camera had captured.

Winston Churchill was quoted as saying , "Never, Never Give Up!" It is great advice. That day, however, my sister-in-law's admonition, "There's One!" really took the cake.

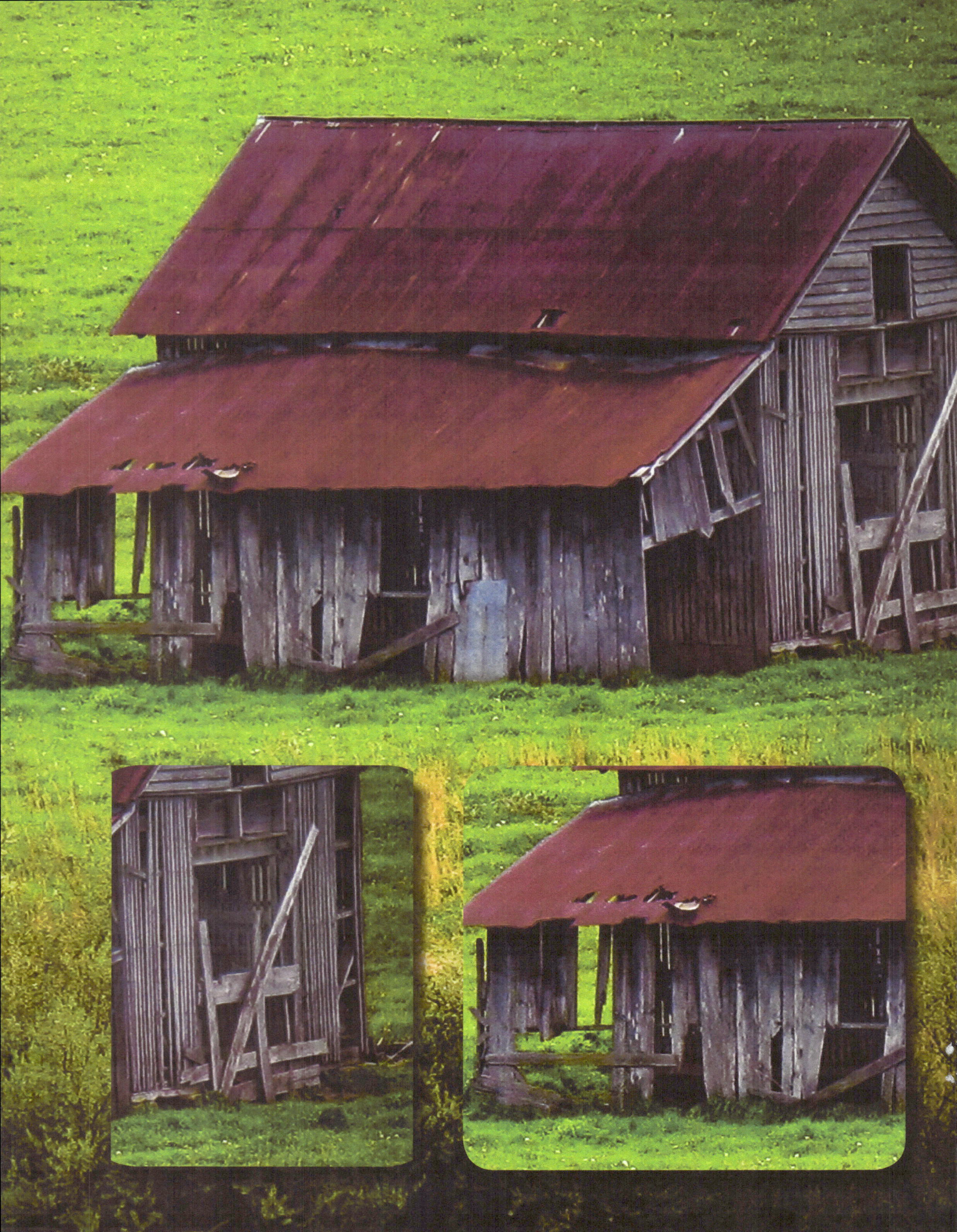

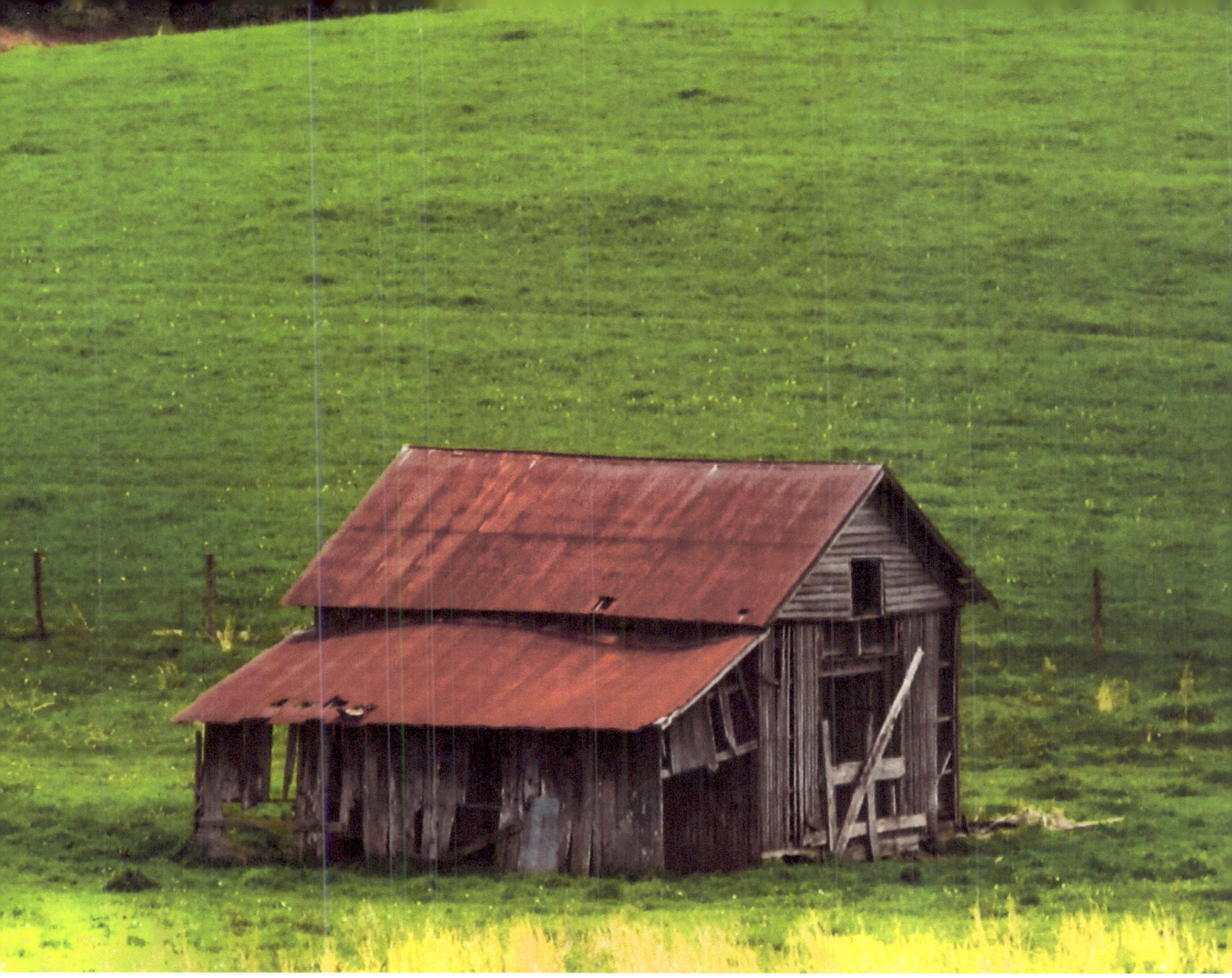

Old Barns Just Fall Apart

I was on the interstate just ready to leave Virginia and head into North Carolina, when off to the side I saw this wonderful setting of an awesome, sprawling old tree and a worn out barn behind it. For a split second I thought about stopping, taking a few shots from my camera, but, it was too late and I moved on, regretting that I had not stopped. I vowed that the next time through, I would "shoot" that scene.

Months later, as I traveled that same interstate and came near to where that scene had been, this old barn on a hill caught my eye. Hurriedly I pulled over to the side, climbed over the railing and took some photographs.

I often ask myself questions when I take such shots. Why was this barn left to decay? Why was it so stark alone, in and amongst a huge field, with no house nearby. What had it been used for? Was that where hay for the cattle had been stored because the barn near the house (if there was one,) was so far away? What events had that barn lived through? How many families had owned that Virginia farm, or was it held by one family throughout the years?

Nestled away from the hustling and bustling interstate, this barn had stood the test of time. It says, "I'm still here, through the storms, the baking sun, the whistling wind off the hillside. I may be tattered, and broken, ... but I'm still here!"

We need to learn from the barn. No matter what comes our way. No matter the storms of life. We need to remain standing, even if we are feeling tattered and broken. If we do, like this old barn scene, someone will still see us as beautiful.

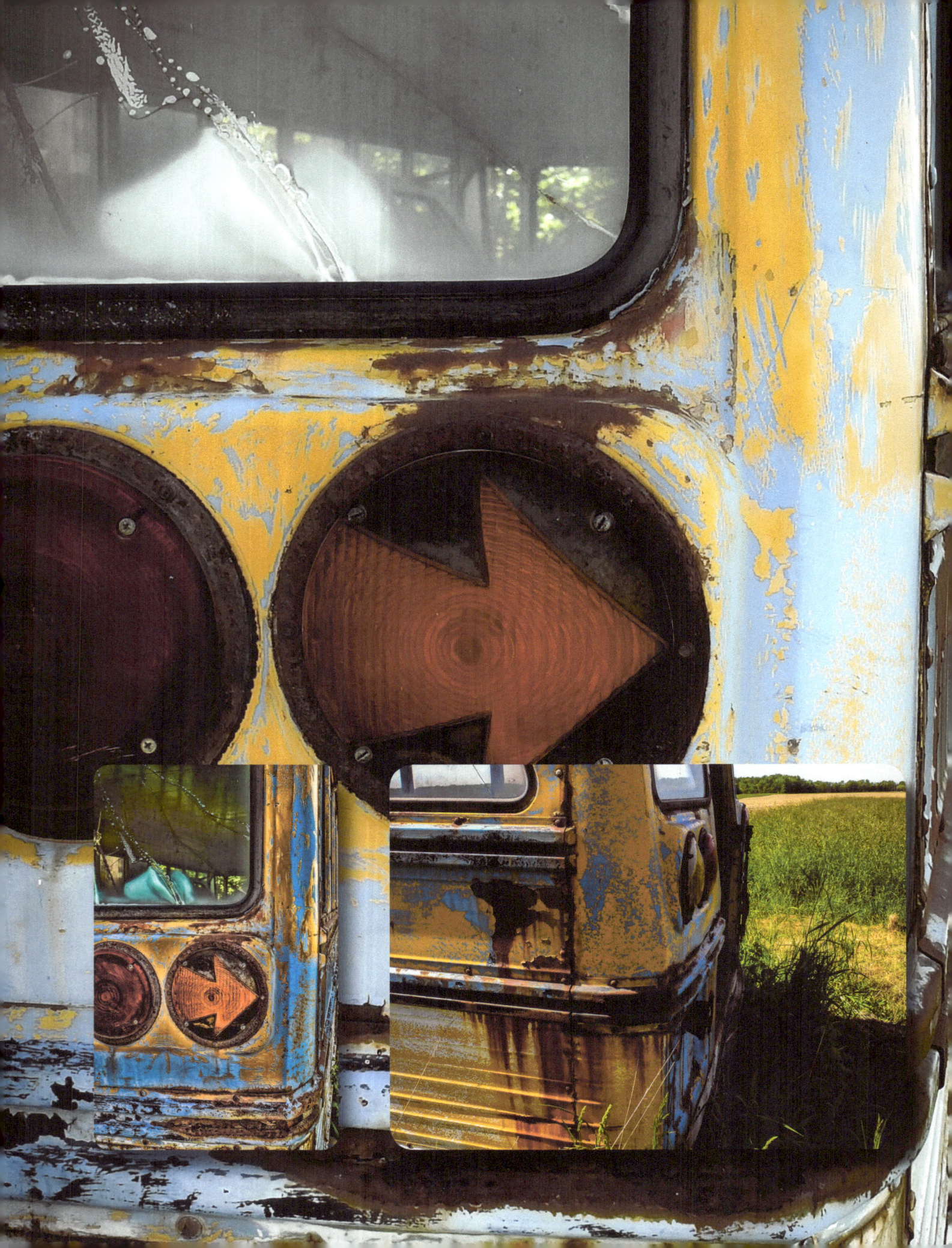

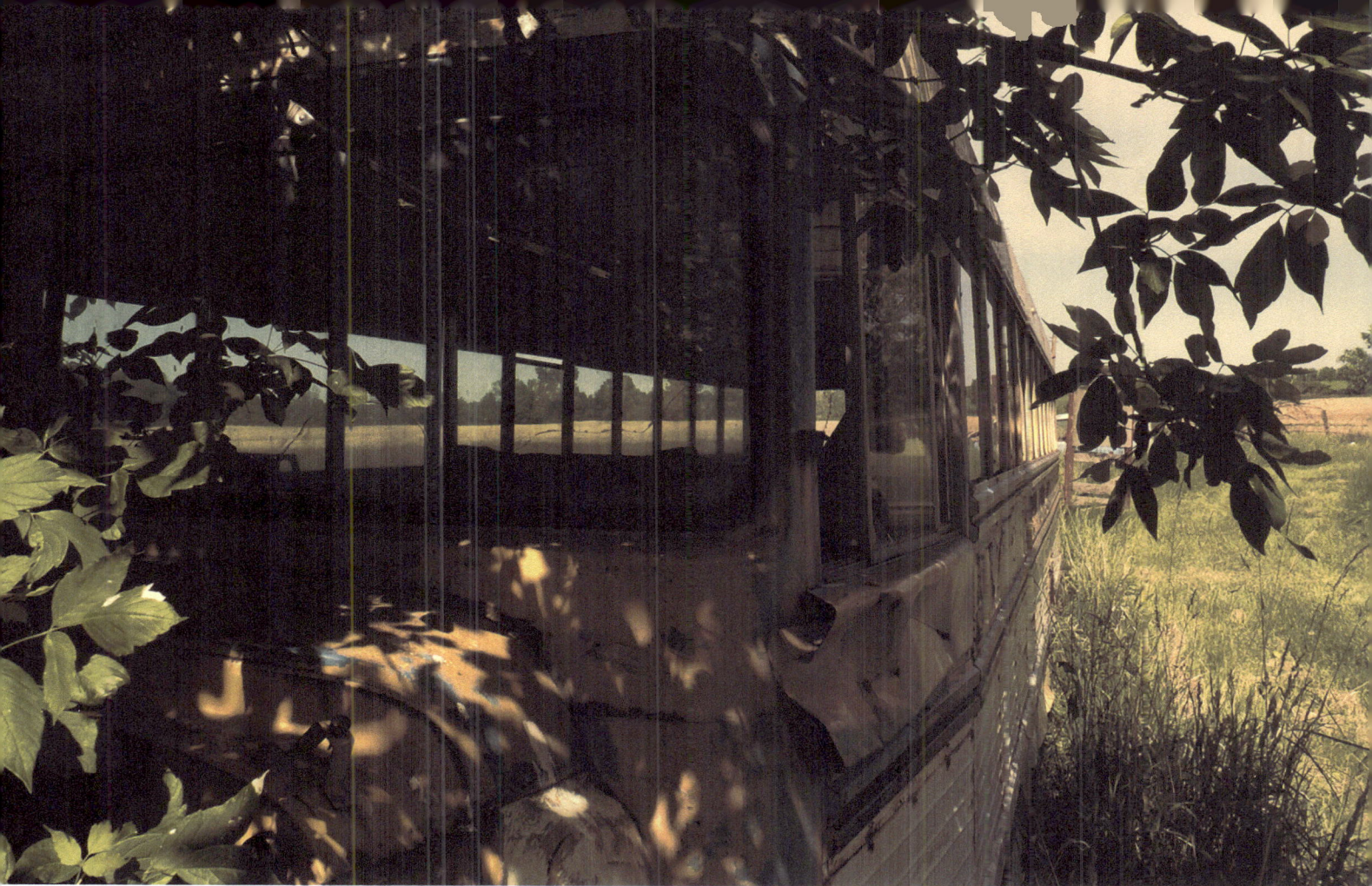

Deserted! ...No Longer Carrying Children

The old farmer had agreed to let me photograph some of the old vehicles he had on his property. The old bus caught my attention, right away. It had been sitting there for some time, being used as a catch-all storage area for the amazing amount of stuff (junk) he had sitting around.

I was captured by this old bus. Never to carry children again. Never to turn its turn signals on or its flashing lights to warn that it had stopped for a precious child.

Much of the color had worn off. It had not been there a short time. Windows were cracked, tires were flat long ago. But what wonderful character it held. Sitting there proud to have served, sad to be in the state it was in. Hidden behind the barn the children couldn't even see it, let alone ride in it.

Some day in the near future it was destined to go to the scrap yard. And then, this relic from the past would be gone! Yet, it had been useful for many years. It had carried children to and from school, to sporting events, band concerts, and field trips. There had been laughter and tears in this old bus. Oh, the stories IT could tell, if it only could.

Maybe it had carried at one time a little boy who had grown up to be a university president, or a little girl who had become a physician. Maybe it had carried a young teen who had become a hero in a war and unfortunately paid the ultimate sacrifice.

As I took the multitude of photographs that day of this bus I felt honored and humbled to be able to record just a small part of history. Who knows what little minds were developed that made or will make major decisions in future years that influence our world for a lifetime. We may never know the full impact of this bus.

And now, I wonder. As we stop for a bus that has flashing caution and red lights, do we think about the huge potential that is riding in those seats today? Or, do we grumble, because that bus may be making us late for an appointment?

I wonder....

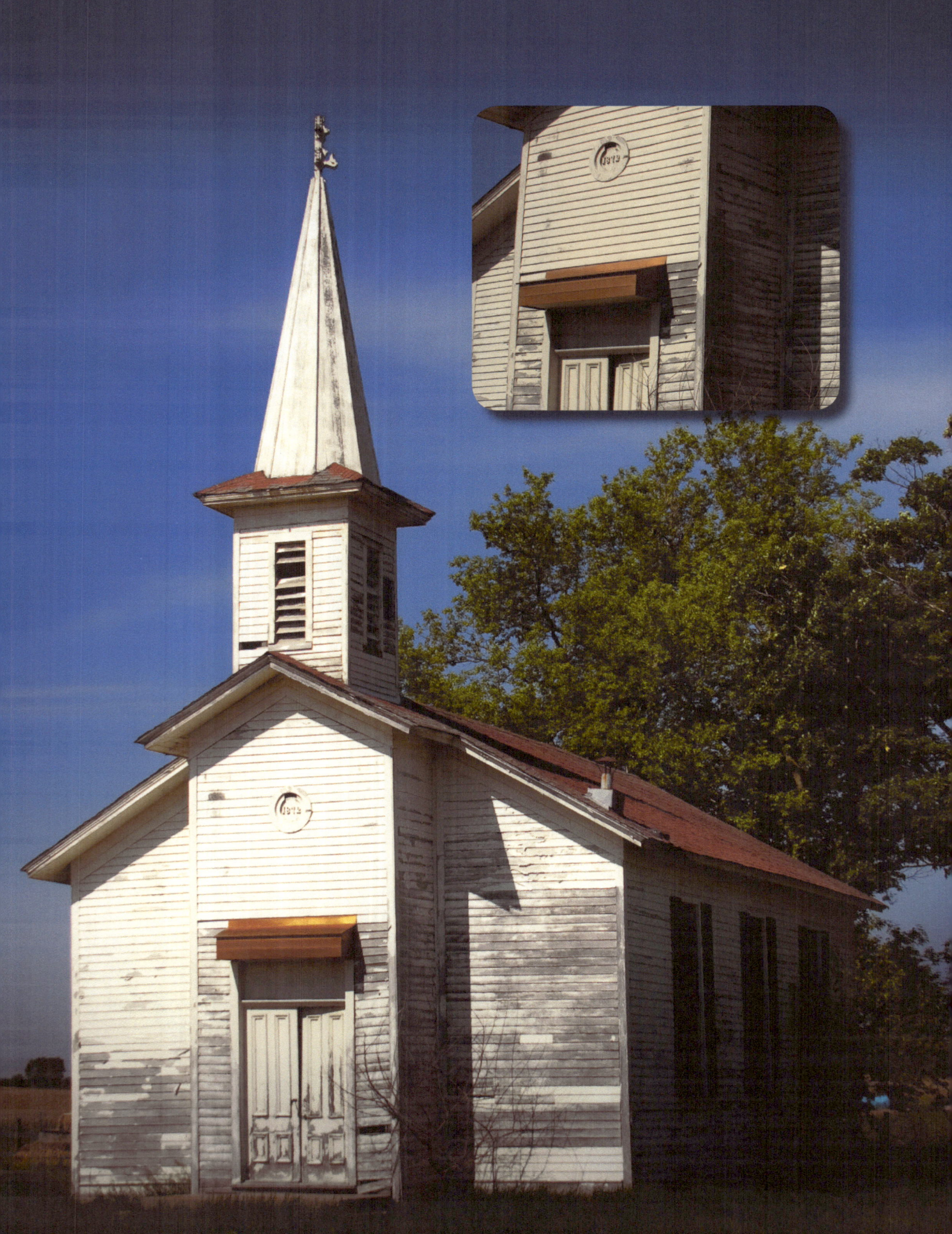

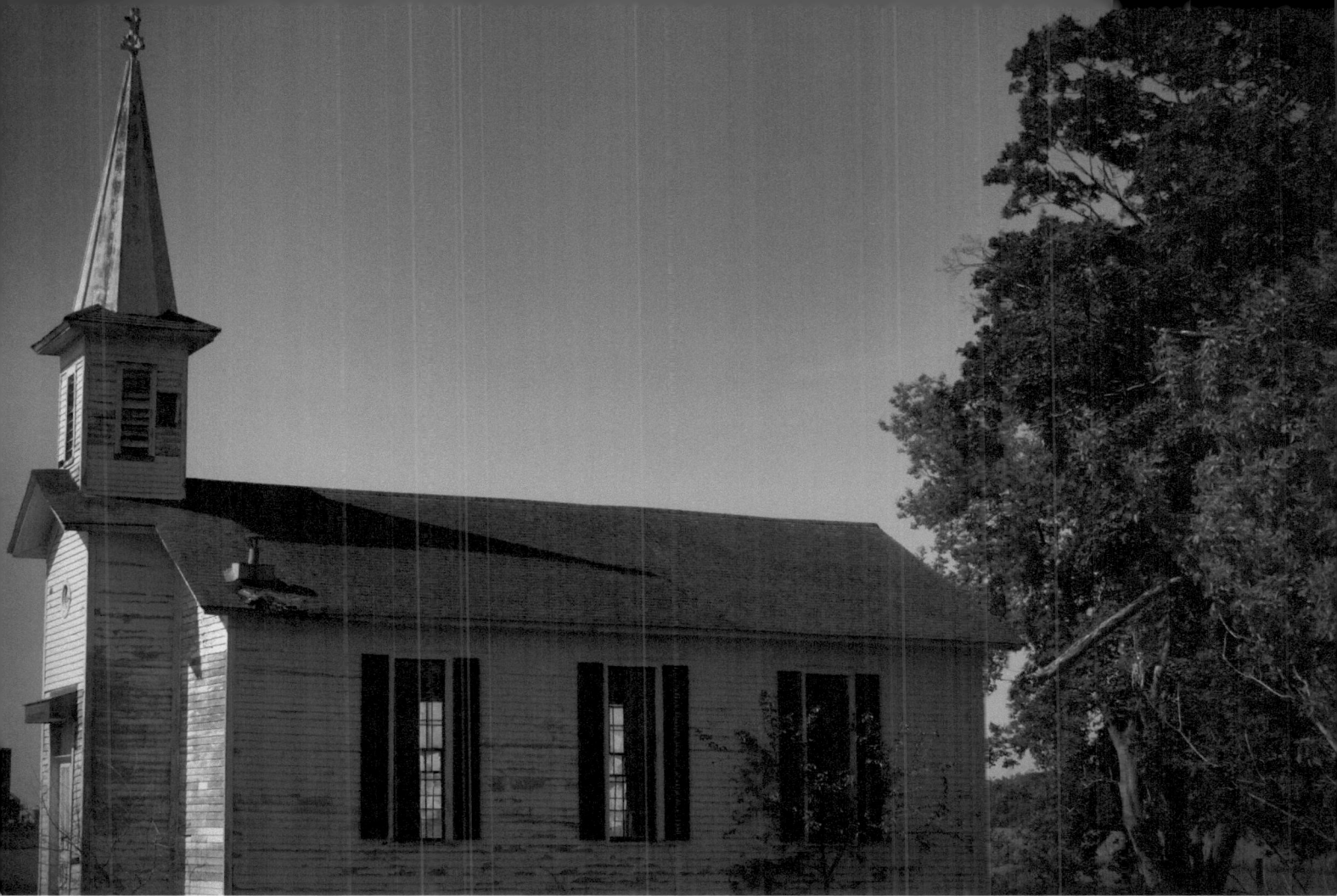

Discarded Church

I had been with Bryan, Chris and the grandkids all weekend and was heading home. Hungry, I saw a Frisch's Big Boy Restaurant sign on the inter-state highway and knew that it would have a breakfast buffet. Turning off the freeway, onto the state road I saw it. I was totally captivated. I had to stop to photograph this once proud, truly gorgeous church in the middle of no-where (except for the interstate highway.)

But the years and the circumstances had taken its toll. Now the doors were slightly open, windows broken out, paint peeling off the rotting wood. The steeple, still reaching for the sky was missing slat after slat where the bell had once been.

It was beautiful, or once had been, but it was all so tragic, as well. I wondered what had happened to the generations of families that had called the country church "their" church home. What about the young couples, deep in love, that had repeated their sacred vows at the altar of this old country church. Where were they now? Were they still together? What about the families that had lost loved ones there, and the little children who had come to know Jesus there? How many church fights had there been, and how many old fashioned covered dish dinners had there been? What impact had this little 'old country church" had on the lives of future generations?

Progress isn't always what it is cracked up to be. There are casualties along the way. Once beautiful edifices where young and old alike had gathered to worship the Lord, now turned to decay, broken windows, peeling paint and a tear from my eyes.

Maybe it touched me more because I had spent twenty-three years in ministry serving God and His church. Maybe all of those weddings and funerals found their way from the cobwebs of my mind.

How many pastors had preached there? How many lives were "saved" there.

I hope the people didn't give up on the church, even though they gave up on the building, called "that old country church."

11

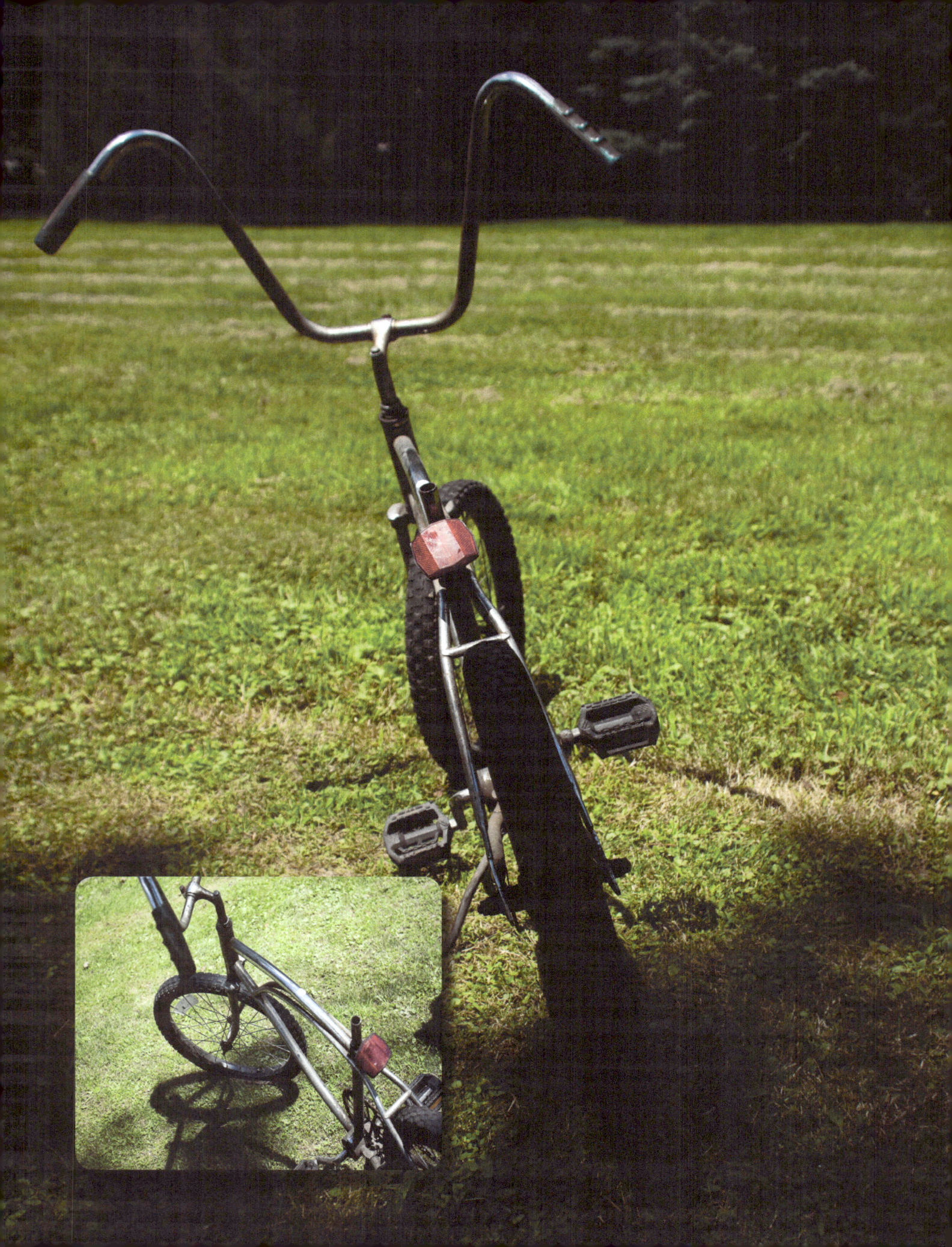

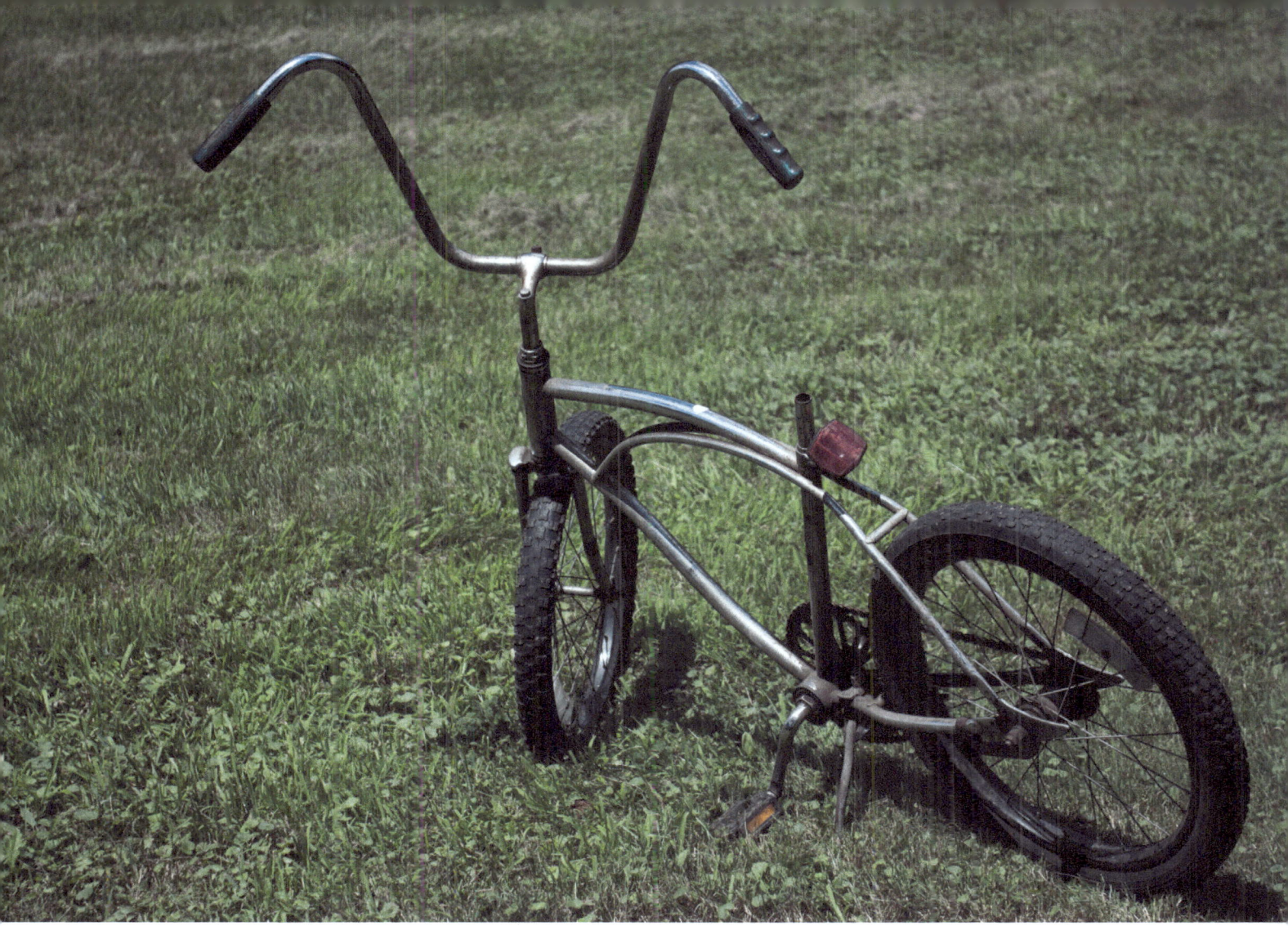

No Longer Popular

It had been sitting at the garage sale since it started days before. At first there were seven or eight cool bikes but now we were down to one. I hadn't paid much attention to this bike at my neighbors garage sale. But just before closing it totally down, the bike became the center of the conversation. Only $5.00, missing a seat, and with flat tires. It really didn't look like something someone would want.

But then I realized what was there. This was a ProMaster bike from the 1970's. At one time it was one of the most popular type bikes for kids (and maybe some adults.) High chrome handlebars, tassels coming out of the handle grips, a beautiful white banana seat and chrome fenders. Who would not have wanted that bike? It would have been a beauty!!

I'm not sure who rode it the most but it had been part of a family for forty years, give or take. And now, ...now it was a cast-away.

To be frank, I was tempted to save it, polish what was left of the chrome, fix the tires, put a beautiful banana seat from Ebay back on it and present it to one of our grandchildren. ....But then, ... I walked away.

I still wonder if I should have saved it from going to the junk pile. Maybe they would have taken $2.00 for it. But it really wasn't the money. I just made a choice to let it go. Certainly next year it won't be back for the yearly neighborhood garage sale.

We do that, don't we? Make split second choices. Some important. Some not. And sometimes the things that were most popular, are now ready for the junk pile. And we just don't do anything about it, but let it go. Sometimes, however, it may not be the correct choice.

Think about it.

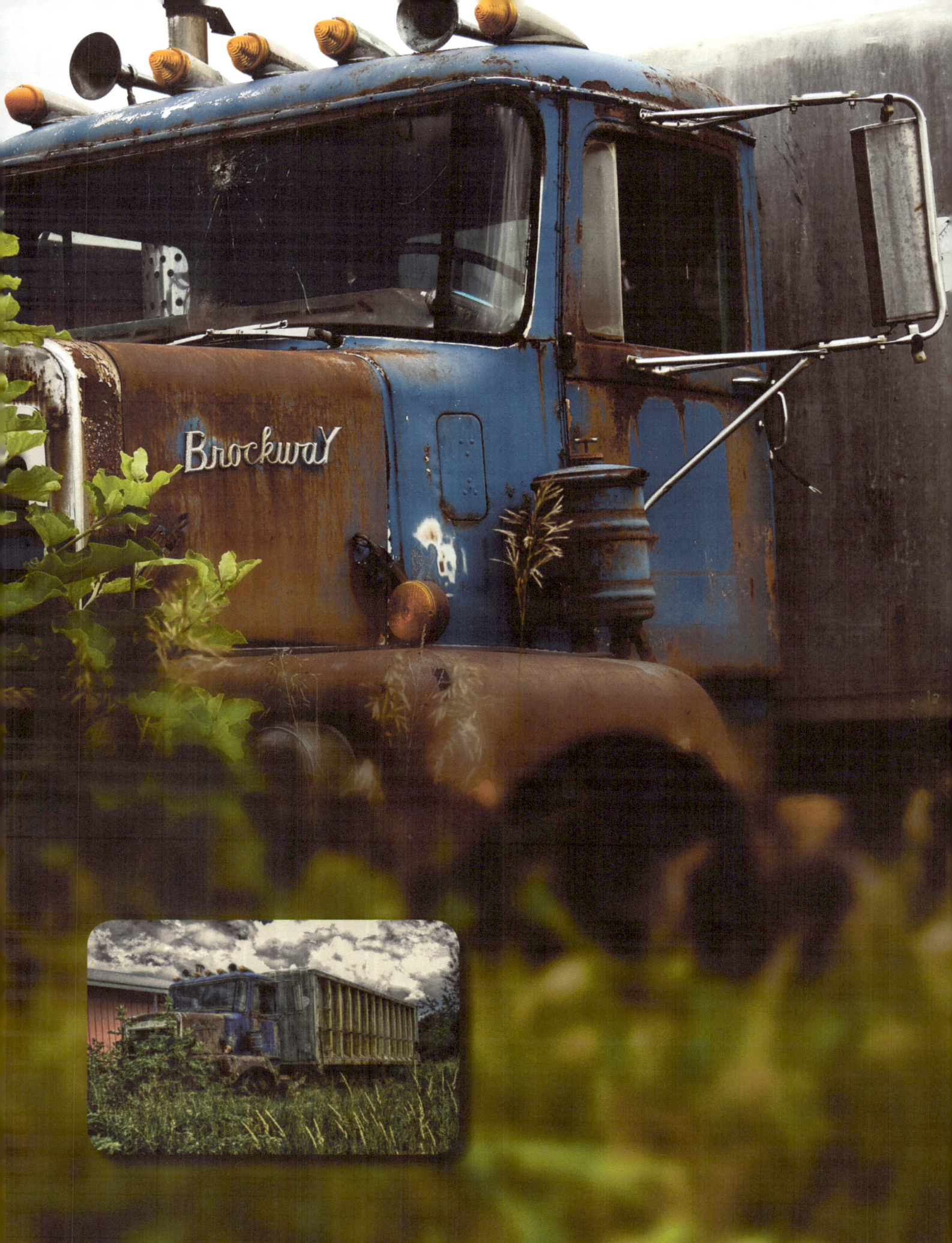

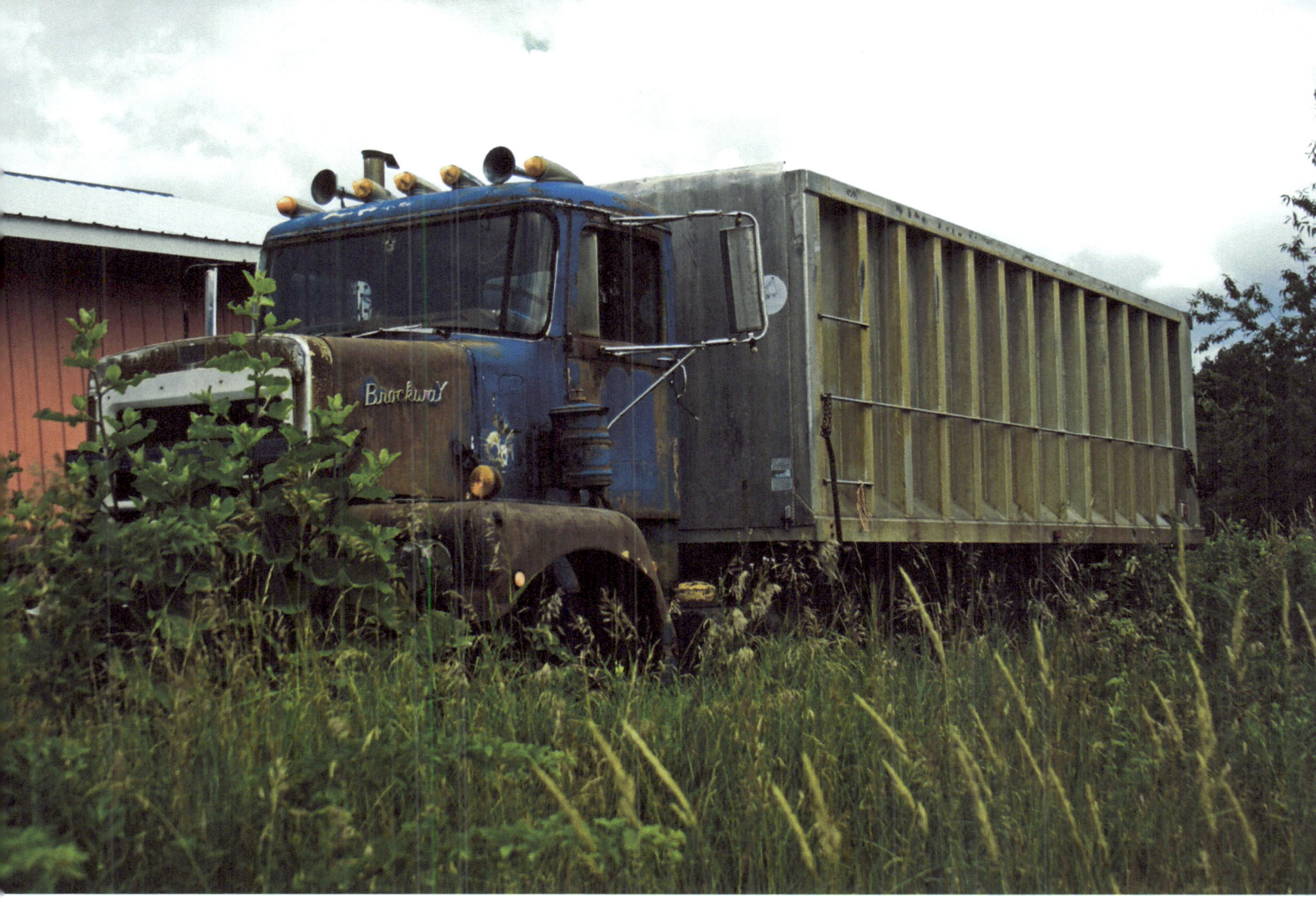

America's "Mighty Big Truck"

Unless you had a reason to use trucks or were an aficionado of the trucking world, you would not know about this truck. Of course, I've heard about Mack, International Harvester, Peterbilt and Kenworth, just to name a few.

But it wasn't until one sunny Saturday afternoon that I ran across this old, rusty, "forgotten" truck of yesteryear. As often happens to old vehicles, no longer in use, it was relegated to the back field (and not a field of dreams, by the way.) Along with other vehicles, it was placed to rot, decay, and be left alone.

Seldom does anyone like me come along to take professional photographs of these "treasures of the past." But this day, my friend Doug and I happened to drive by, and turned around to drive down the side road to see if this was what I wanted to shoot. The closer I got, the more this big truck called out to me, "Take my photograph. Don't let me be forgotten!"

This old truck is a "Brockway." The company started in the late 1800's and finally bit the dust in the 1970's. Brockway's were huge, heavy trucks that could do huge, heavy jobs. In the latter years they were not mass made from an assembly line without a buyer in mind. They were made "to order." From 1912 until their demise in 1977, the Brockway Company made its aim and mission to build quality trucks, and that is what they did. Brockway's were called "The Most Rugged Truck In The World."

Unfortunately, the once Mighty will eventually fall. And so, this truck, sits in a field, gathering rust, and whatever, never to be used again.

Is it possible that we allow the same thing to happen to our dreams and goals in life? We start off strong with wonderful, adventurous dreams and goals, but then, ... Once lofty, "mighty, if you please," they are allowed through the ravages of time "to fall," and be relegated to an old field, not a "field of dreams," but one where the weeds grow up around us and our hopes, dreams and goals begin to "rust, decay, and fall apart on us." Isn't it sad, that we allow that to happen?

15

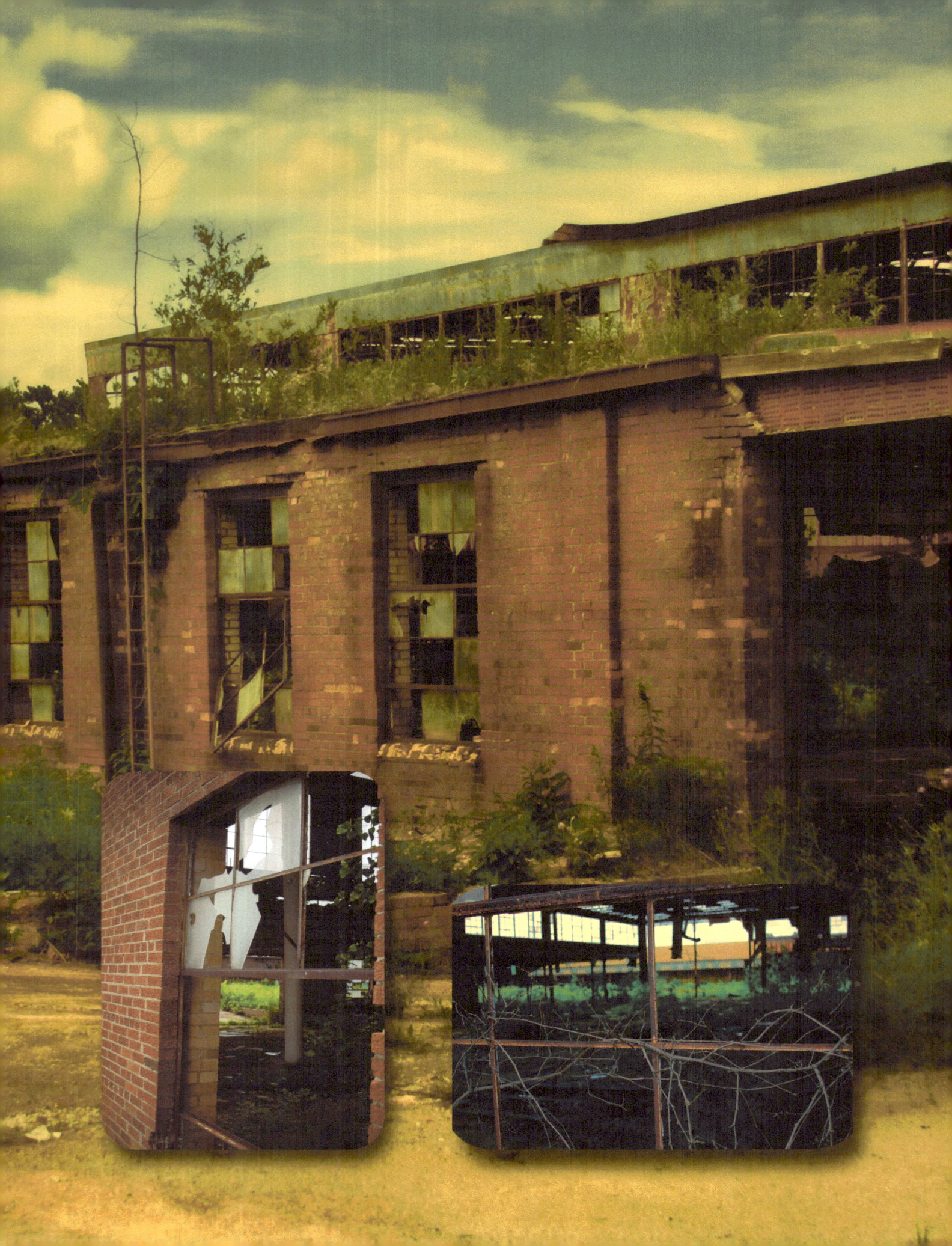

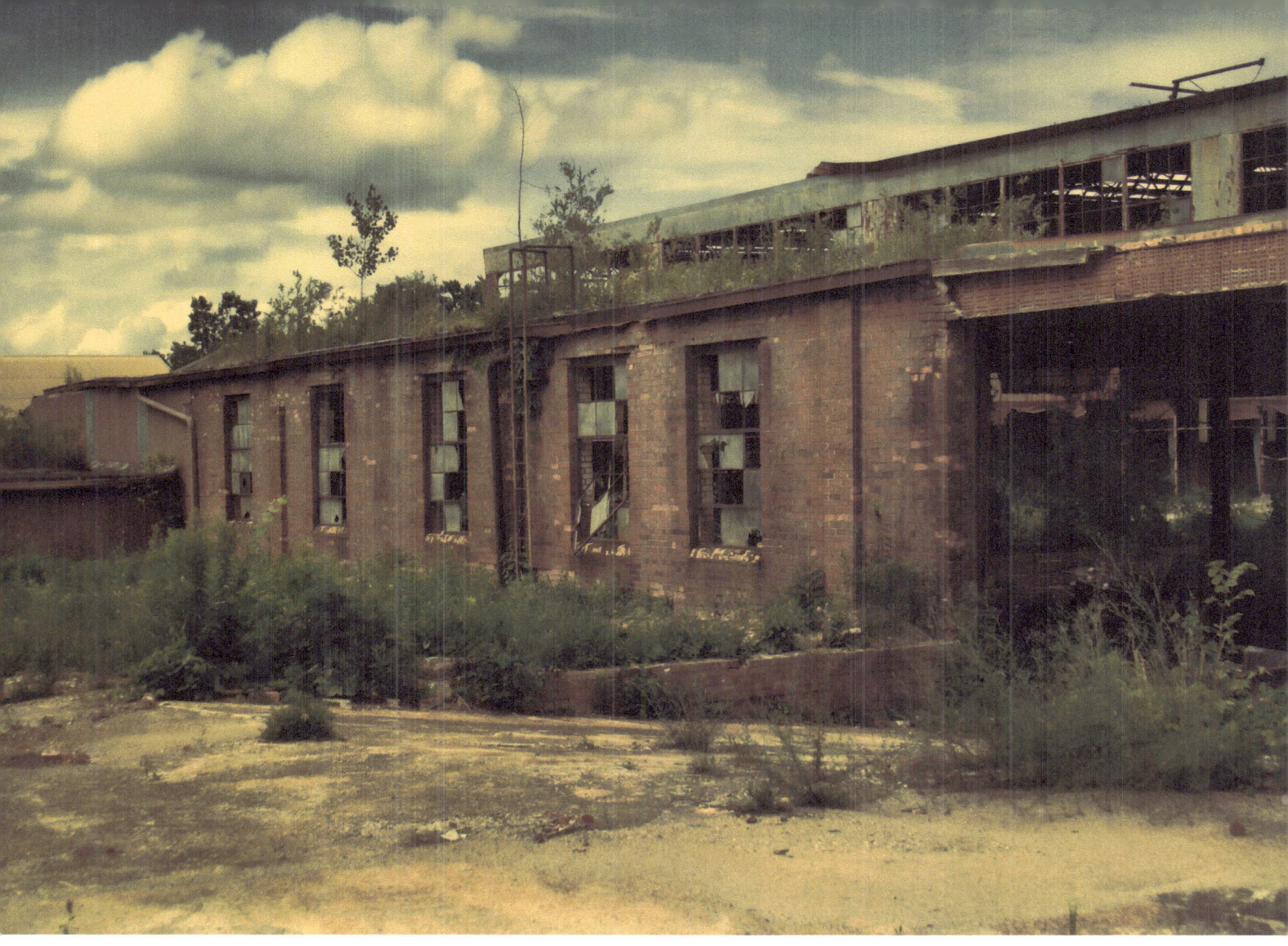

Beyond Its Usefulness

Mansfield, Ohio is over 200 years old, having started in 1808. In the 1800's many of the roads and houses were made of brick. You can still drive a few blocks on brick in one small section of Mansfield. The old brick factory used to be a thriving place and busy making brick for the streets and the buildings of Mansfield. Now, just outside of town, it sits desolate, with the ravages of vandalism and time.

When I first saw this complex of multiple buildings I was captivated not only by the desecration that time has brought to it, but at the same time I was mesmerized by the beauty of the facility, even in its horrible state. There was something that drew me to it, looking through the windows at a building now grown up with weeds and small trees instead of the regular floor. Catching how the building continued to stand in spite of everything that nature could throw at it.

Unfortunately it has gone way beyond its usefulness, except for those few folks who cover the walls with graffiti.

It is sad to know that like so many other things, there are stories that have been lived out there that will never be known or told in the years to come. Many have long since gone to the grave!

On that note, may I say to you, keep the stories alive in your life. Write them down, video yourself (yes, even you) telling your stories so that family and friends who come behind will be able to connect the past with the present. It is sad that way too many people are unaware of the personal history of their families.

We need to return to being a story telling society. It is the bridge that spans the time between the past, the present and the future.

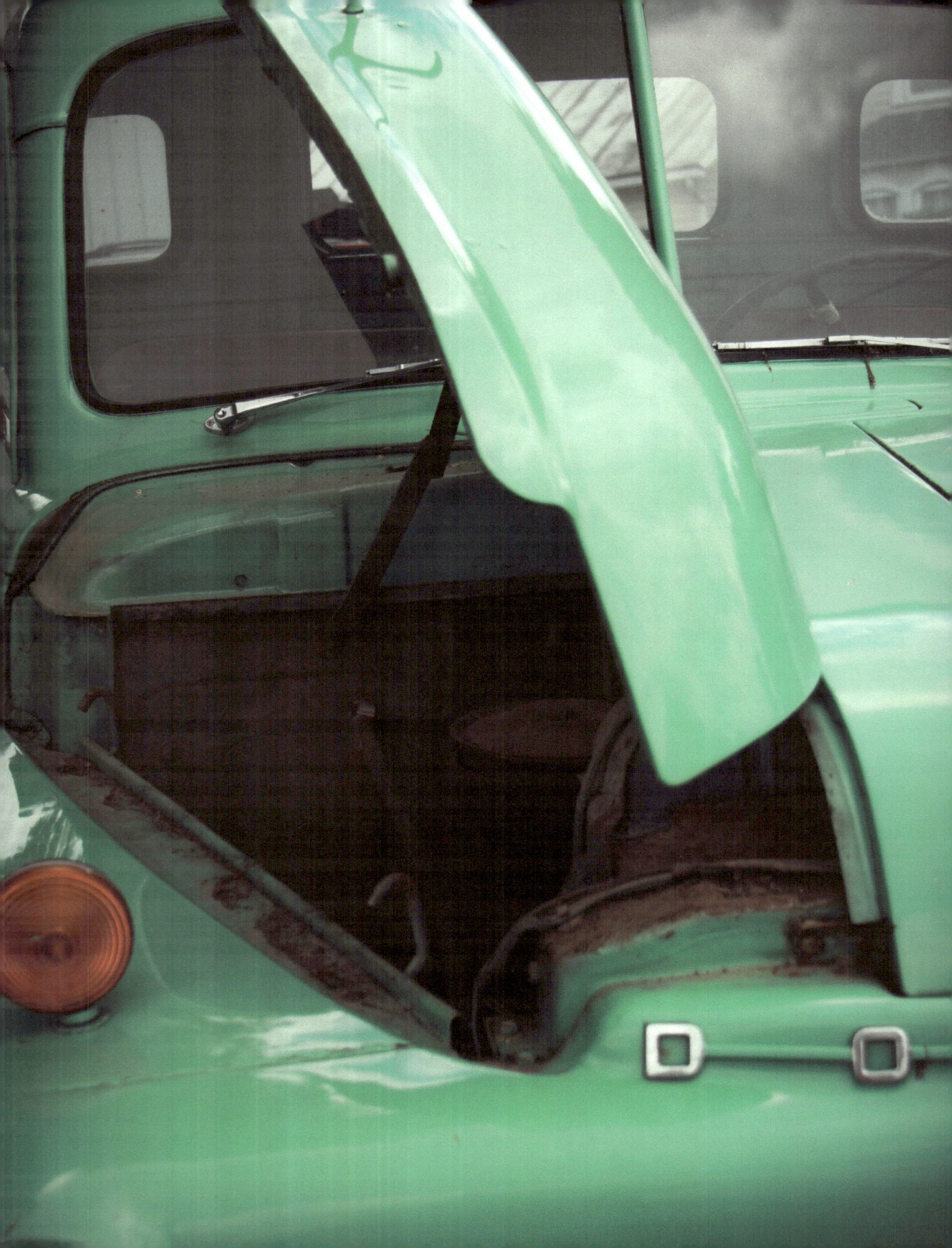

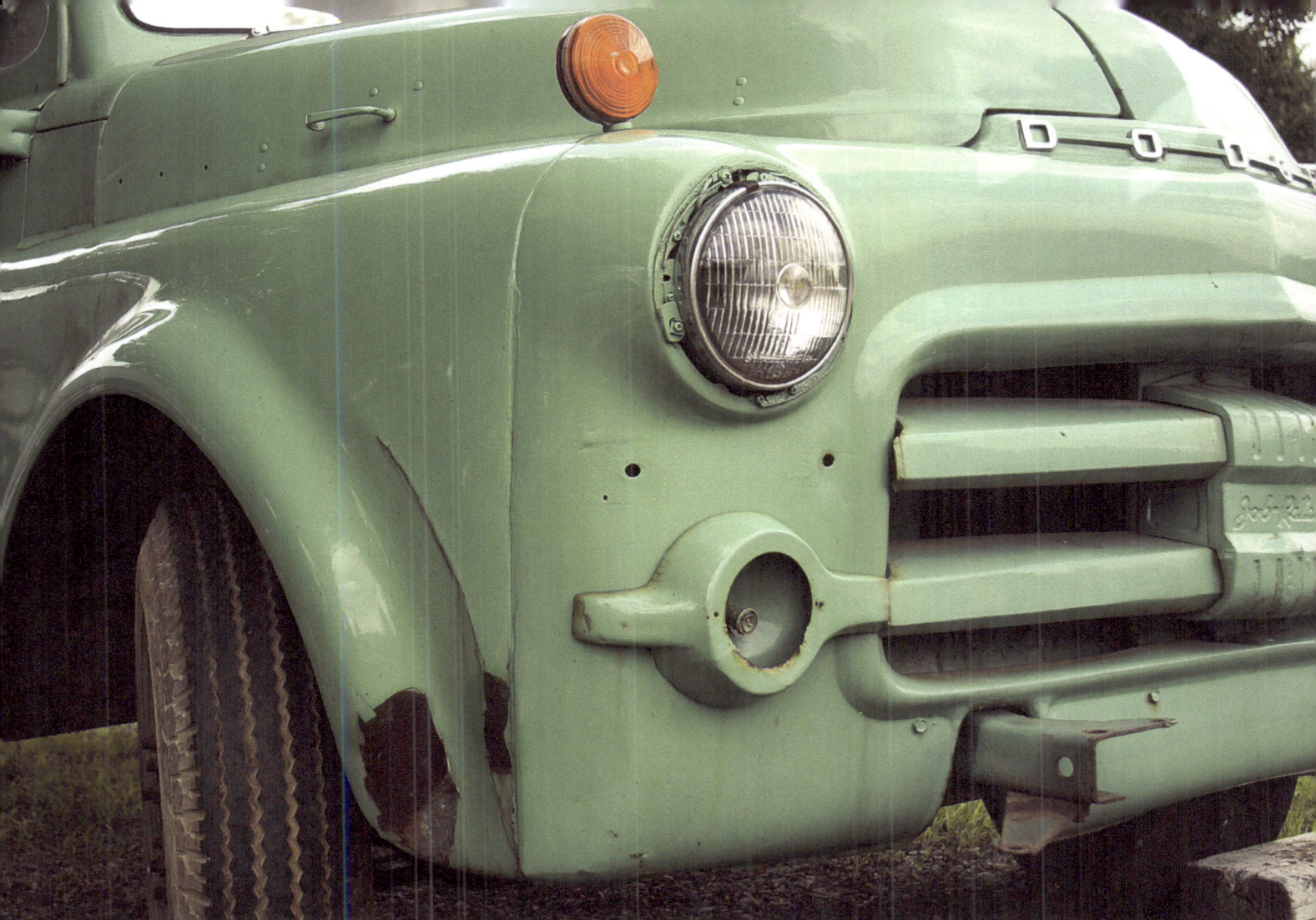

Attempted! ...Yet An Aborted Restoration

There are always things started, but left unaccomplished.

So, it seems that is what happened to this old Dodge truck found along the road, "For Sale," one Saturday afternoon. *Unfinished accomplishments! They are often the story of our lives.*

Someone had attempted, at least in part, to restore this old truck to its "glory years." They had painted it. But that was about it. What happened to stop the restoration we do not know. Was it lack of monetary funds? A divorce? An illness? Boredom setting in?

The minute my friend, Doug, and I saw this old truck as we were driving along the back roads, we just "knew that it was a keeper." It was a story that had to be told photographically. As I looked over this beautiful, but very worn, vehicle, I realized again that unfinished business always comes back to haunt us, and sometimes even makes things worse.

The new (?) paint job wasn't the best one you could find. Certainly the rust on the fender tells us that The fact that the paint isn't even tells us that either someone was in a hurry or didn't know how to do the job. To do it right, this old truck will have to be repainted correctly. And, then, there were the lack of parts. Everywhere you turned this old truck needed parts it did not have.

I don't know about you, but there are some unfinished projects in my life. I need to get to work and finish them. This old Dodge truck reminded me that it is dangerous to attempt, but then abort a restoration project.

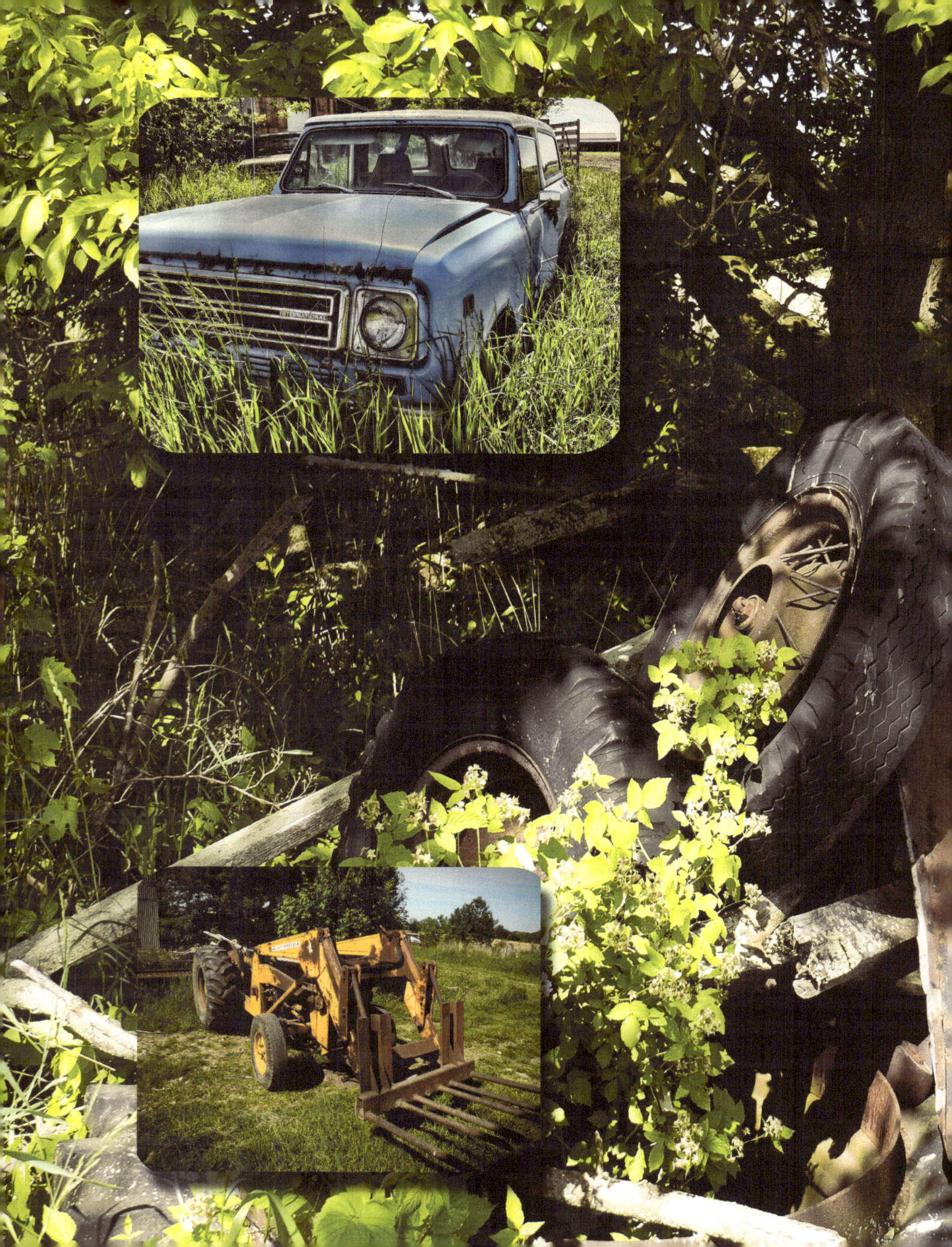

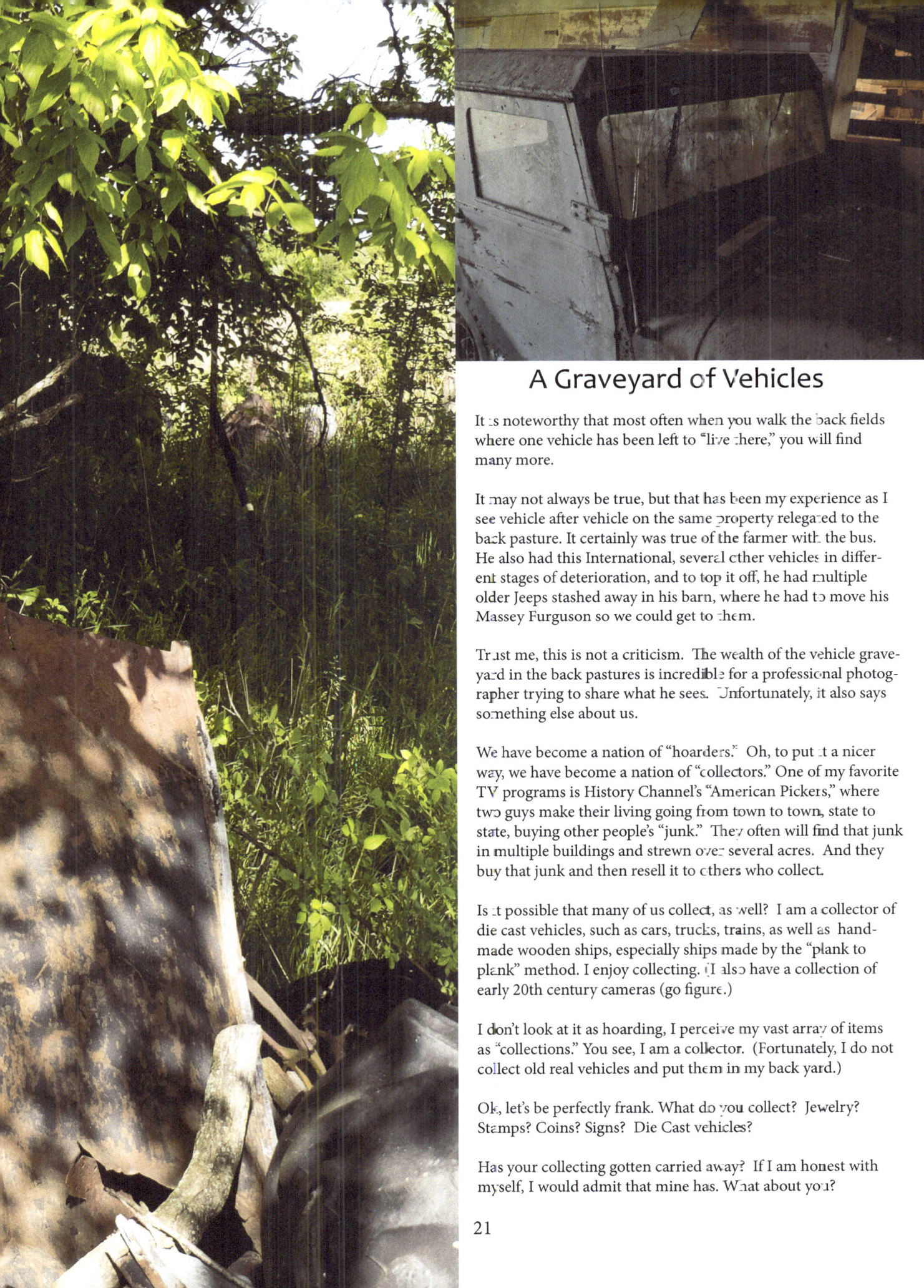

A Graveyard of Vehicles

It is noteworthy that most often when you walk the back fields where one vehicle has been left to "live there," you will find many more.

It may not always be true, but that has been my experience as I see vehicle after vehicle on the same property relegated to the back pasture. It certainly was true of the farmer with the bus. He also had this International, several other vehicles in different stages of deterioration, and to top it off, he had multiple older Jeeps stashed away in his barn, where he had to move his Massey Furguson so we could get to them.

Trust me, this is not a criticism. The wealth of the vehicle graveyard in the back pastures is incredible for a professional photographer trying to share what he sees. Unfortunately, it also says something else about us.

We have become a nation of "hoarders." Oh, to put it a nicer way, we have become a nation of "collectors." One of my favorite TV programs is History Channel's "American Pickers," where two guys make their living going from town to town, state to state, buying other people's "junk." They often will find that junk in multiple buildings and strewn over several acres. And they buy that junk and then resell it to others who collect.

Is it possible that many of us collect, as well? I am a collector of die cast vehicles, such as cars, trucks, trains, as well as handmade wooden ships, especially ships made by the "plank to plank" method. I enjoy collecting. (I also have a collection of early 20th century cameras (go figure.)

I don't look at it as hoarding, I perceive my vast array of items as "collections." You see, I am a collector. (Fortunately, I do not collect old real vehicles and put them in my back yard.)

Ok, let's be perfectly frank. What do you collect? Jewelry? Stamps? Coins? Signs? Die Cast vehicles?

Has your collecting gotten carried away? If I am honest with myself, I would admit that mine has. What about you?

21

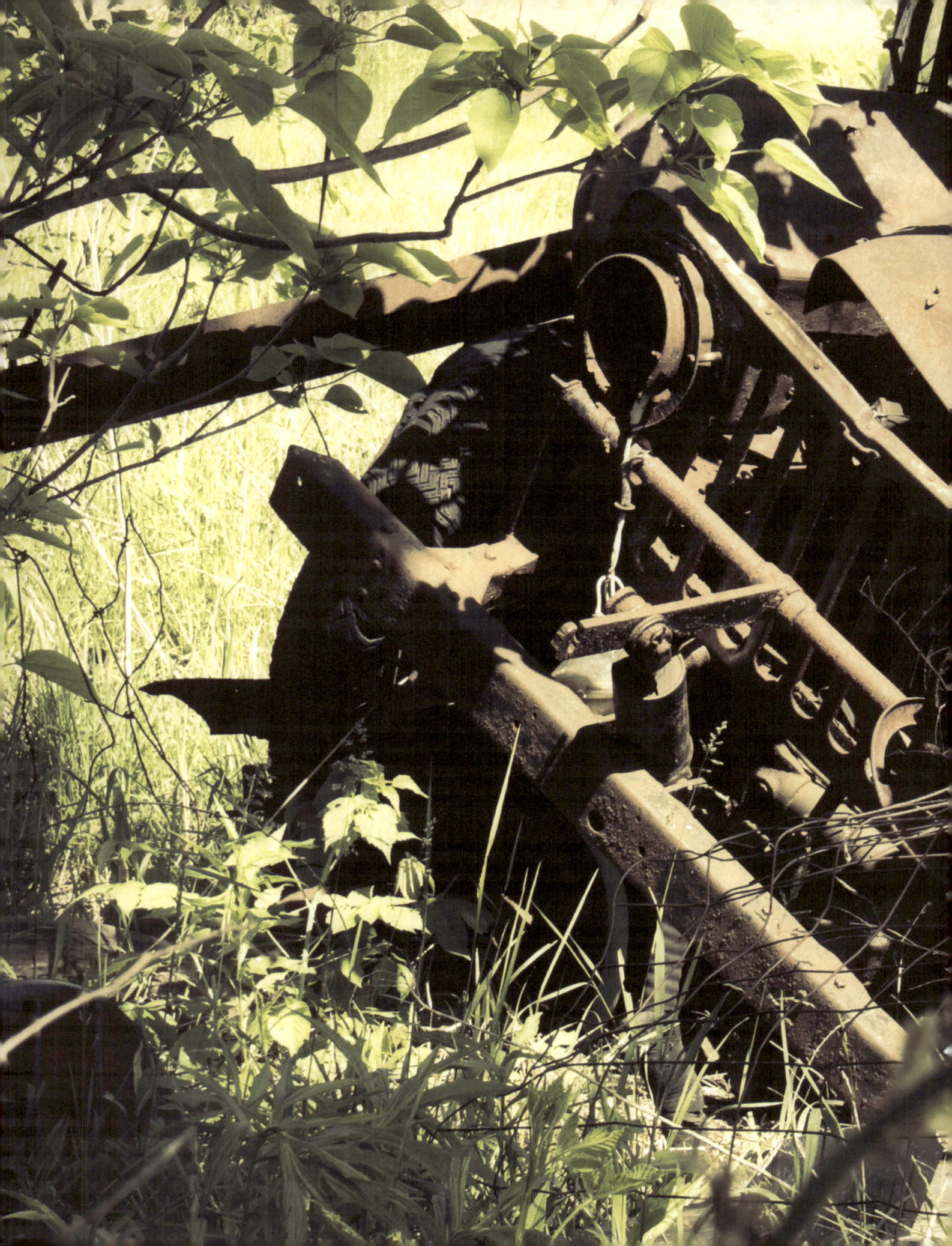

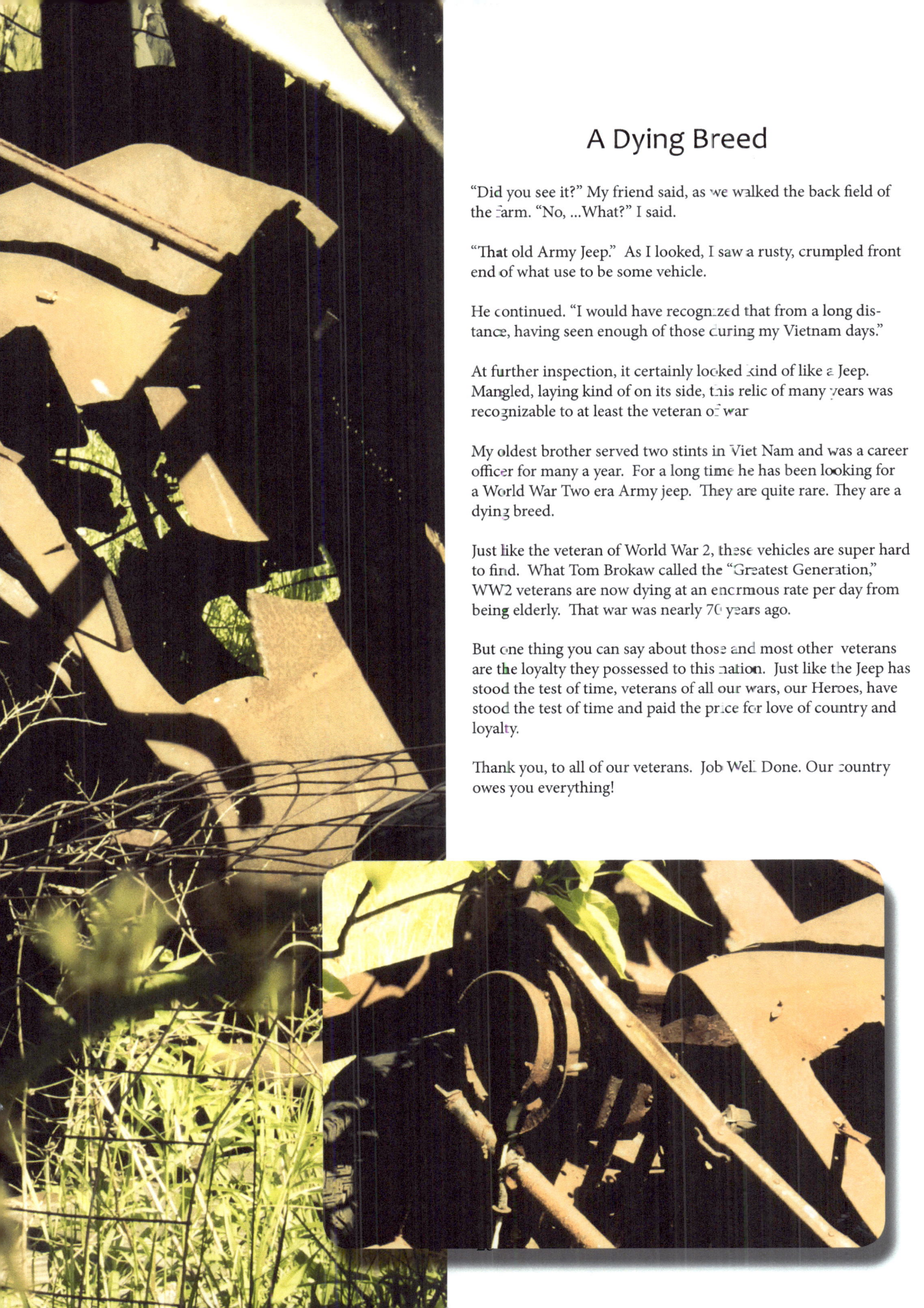

A Dying Breed

"Did you see it?" My friend said, as we walked the back field of the farm. "No, ...What?" I said.

"That old Army Jeep." As I looked, I saw a rusty, crumpled front end of what use to be some vehicle.

He continued. "I would have recognized that from a long distance, having seen enough of those during my Vietnam days."

At further inspection, it certainly looked kind of like a Jeep. Mangled, laying kind of on its side, this relic of many years was recognizable to at least the veteran of war

My oldest brother served two stints in Viet Nam and was a career officer for many a year. For a long time he has been looking for a World War Two era Army jeep. They are quite rare. They are a dying breed.

Just like the veteran of World War 2, these vehicles are super hard to find. What Tom Brokaw called the "Greatest Generation," WW2 veterans are now dying at an enormous rate per day from being elderly. That war was nearly 70 years ago.

But one thing you can say about those and most other veterans are the loyalty they possessed to this nation. Just like the Jeep has stood the test of time, veterans of all our wars, our Heroes, have stood the test of time and paid the price for love of country and loyalty.

Thank you, to all of our veterans. Job Well Done. Our country owes you everything!

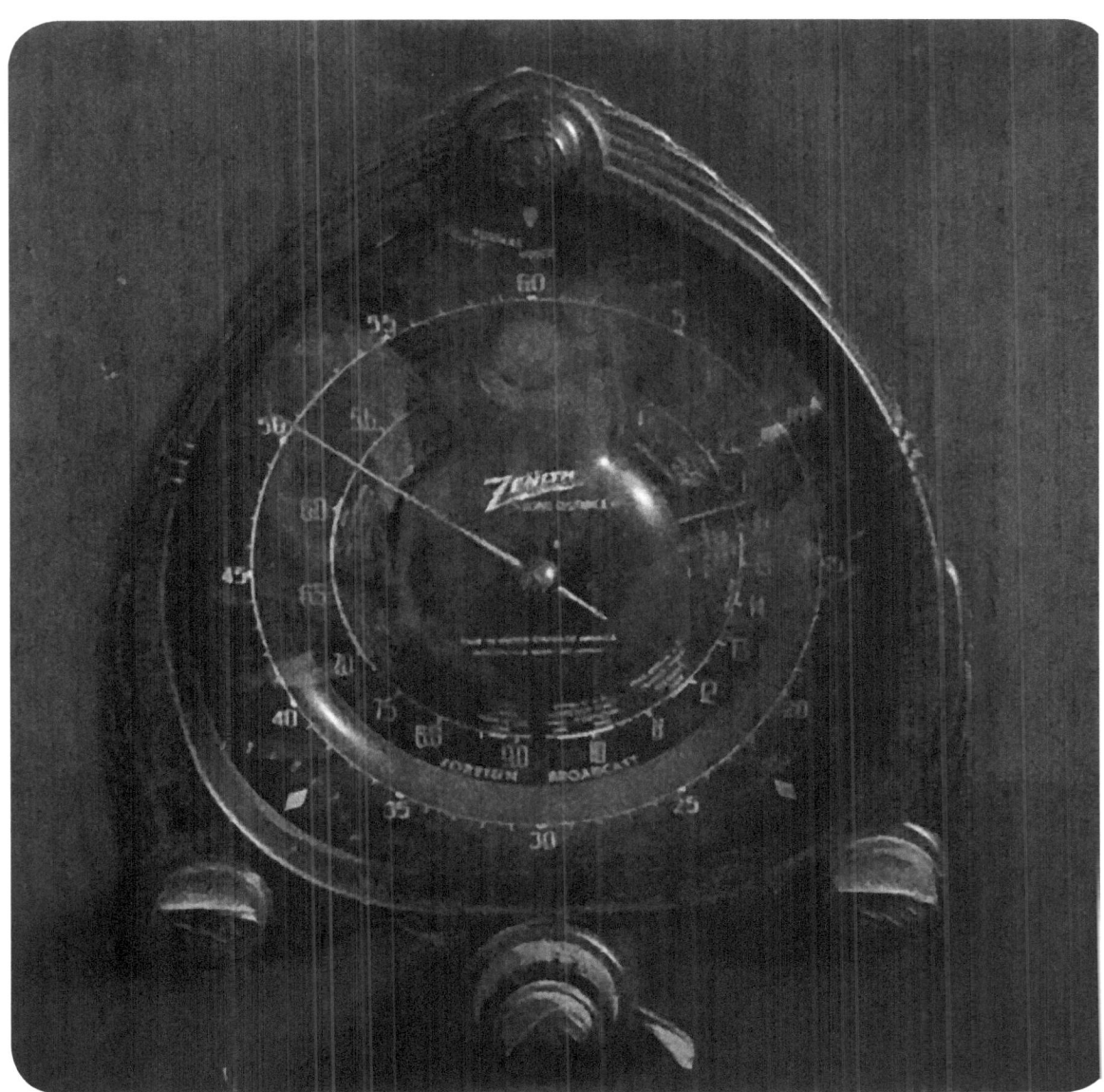

It's Pretty. ...But Does Not Work!

It's in my own home. Belonged to my Grandmother Houtz. One of the only things I requested of her was this beautiful Zenith Shutter Dial Floor model.

It's been around a long time. The company started in 1918, and I'm not sure when this model was built, but I can just imagine my Grandma Ruth and my "old" (to a very young boy,) Grandpa John, sitting around the radio listening to President Roosevelt proclaim the "Day of Infamy."

I've always been fond of this old radio. We must have had it close to forty years, by now. But, as beautiful as it is, and as wonderful an antique that it is, it does not work.

Even in my own home I have "useless things." Nice to look at, (which I hardly ever do, since it is in a room I do not use very often), yet it won't utter a sound.

Until the television came on the scene, the radio was the primary mass communication device. It was vital to a nation, to a community, to a family.

The radio, too, is going the way of the other things in this book. (I have one or two going to a garage sale tomorrow.)

The motto Zenith used for years was, "The quality goes in, before the name goes on." It no longer matters what kind of quality if it doesn't work any longer.

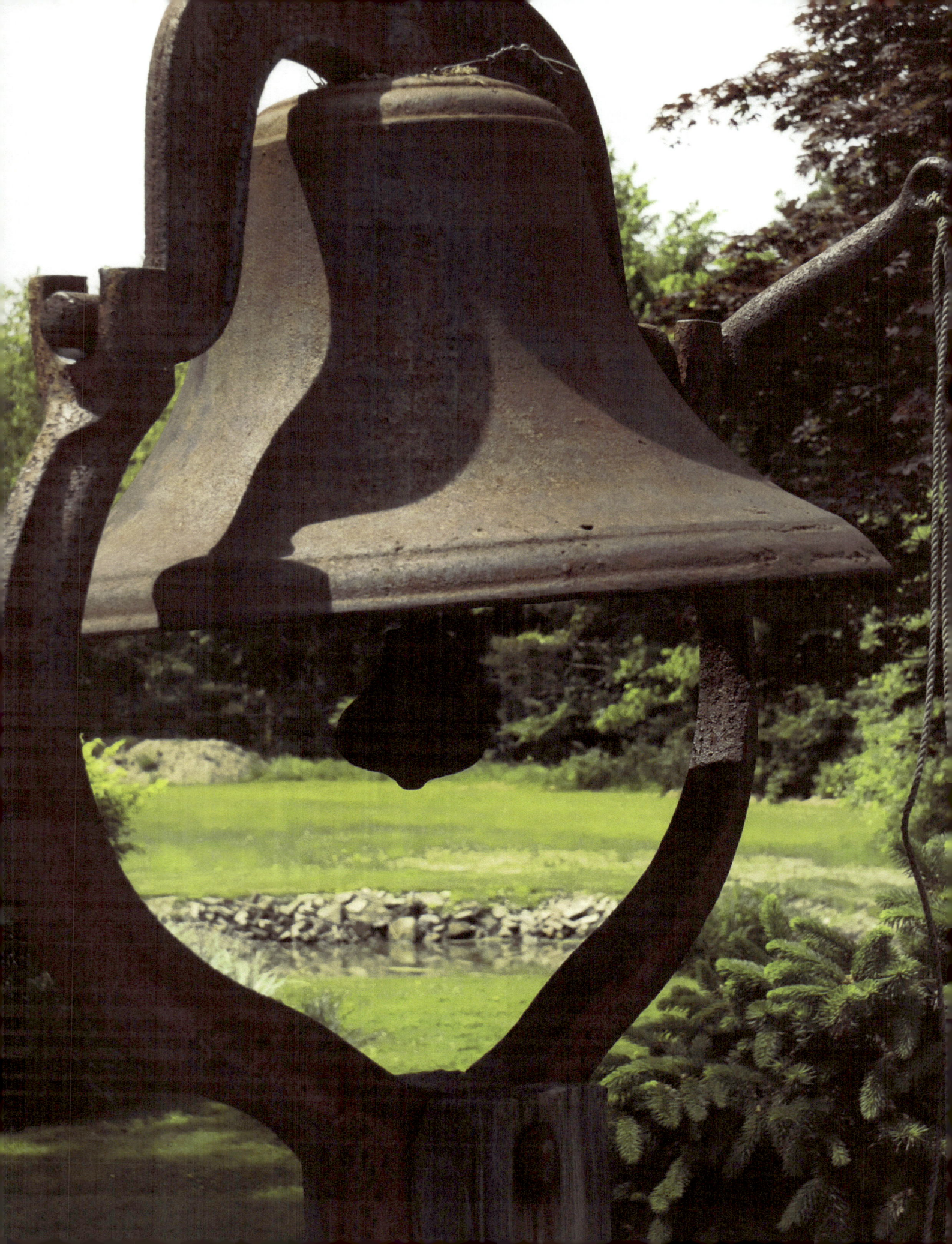

"Rusty" Is In...

This old bell used to be a bright bronze and beautiful, to boot. Through the years it has been attacked by the wrath of time and what was a gorgeous bronze has become, in many ways, a beautiful rust.

It was rescued by my friend, Doug, and his wife Muriel (Lannie.) Doug is a horticulturalist and was a wonderful landscape artist for many years.

Outdoors has been, and is his life. And as the years bring him and I older by the day, this old bell reminds us that even when age attacks, it is still possible to be useful and productive in life. You see, this old bell is not there just to look good and remind one of past glory days, but is quite useful even today.

In the past few years I have broken my hip a couple of times and finally had it replaced with a new one. Then, last fall, I fell down two steps, landing on my knee and breaking my femur into 11 different pieces. Thus, began some six plus months of healing and rehabilitation.

Why do I tell you about this? As we get older our bodies begin to wear and "rust" begins to show. But that doesn't mean that we are ready for the "refuse pile of life." What it does mean is that even though we may move slower, or with a limp, or wear out a little faster than years ago, we can still be productive.

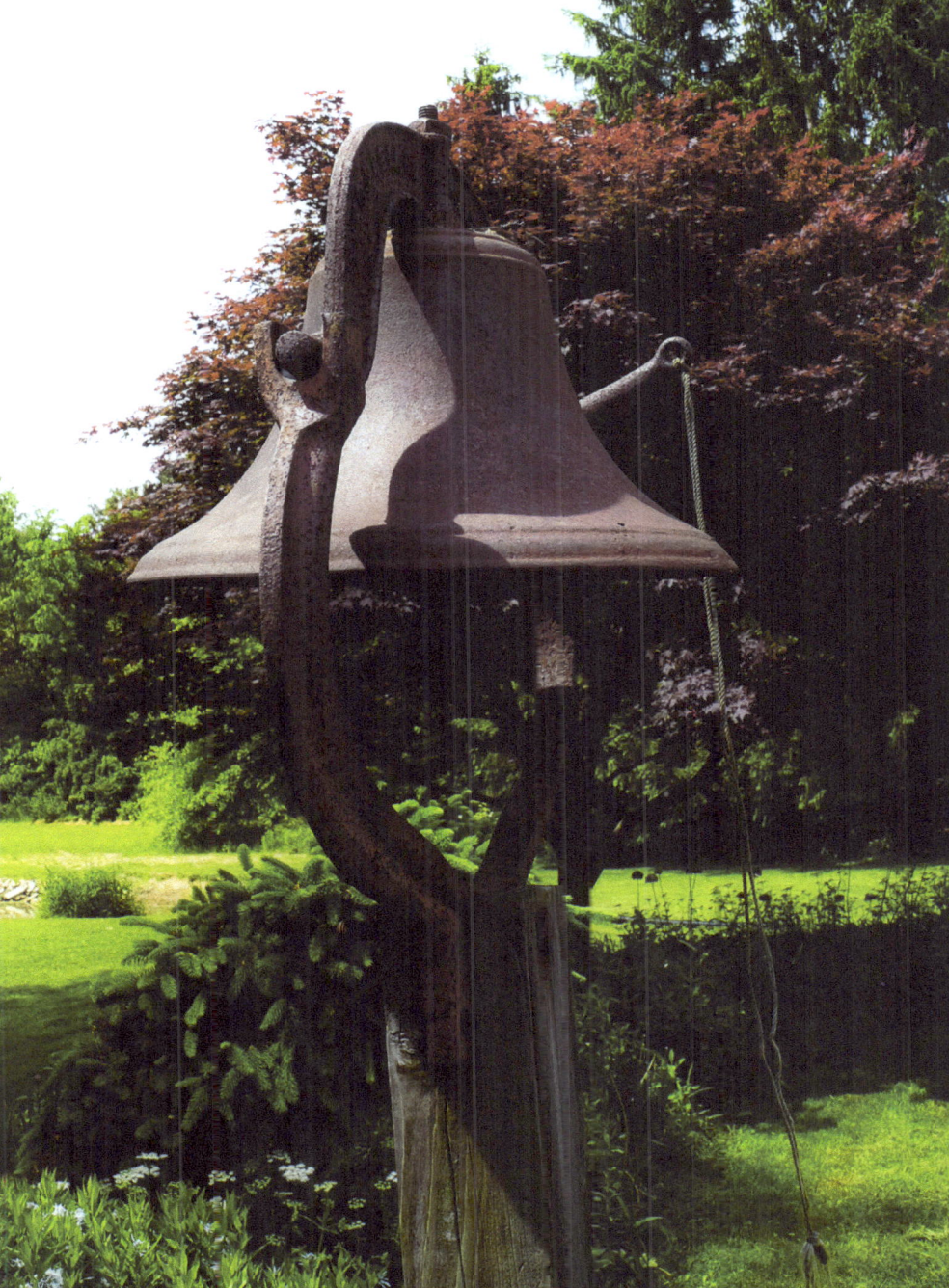

I recently heard a report that those who retire early have a possible higher possibility of dementia because they tend not to use their brain and thought processes as much. Not sure if that is true but it certainly makes sense.

Just before I turned 60 years old, I began my first business that went national in less than two years. Pretty incredible! Past sixty-five now, I own two businesses full time and our photography business expanded into three states in less than seven months. I have written a number of books in the last eight years and my mind is keen, full of dreams and ideas and possibilities.

Time does have its affect on us. It can attack our body and even our minds if we let it. Or, we can remain productive well into our older adult years.

Yes, the bell still rings. True and right on and calls us to action even if the bronze has tarnished and weather has rusted that old bell. Will you be ready to act no matter when called upon?

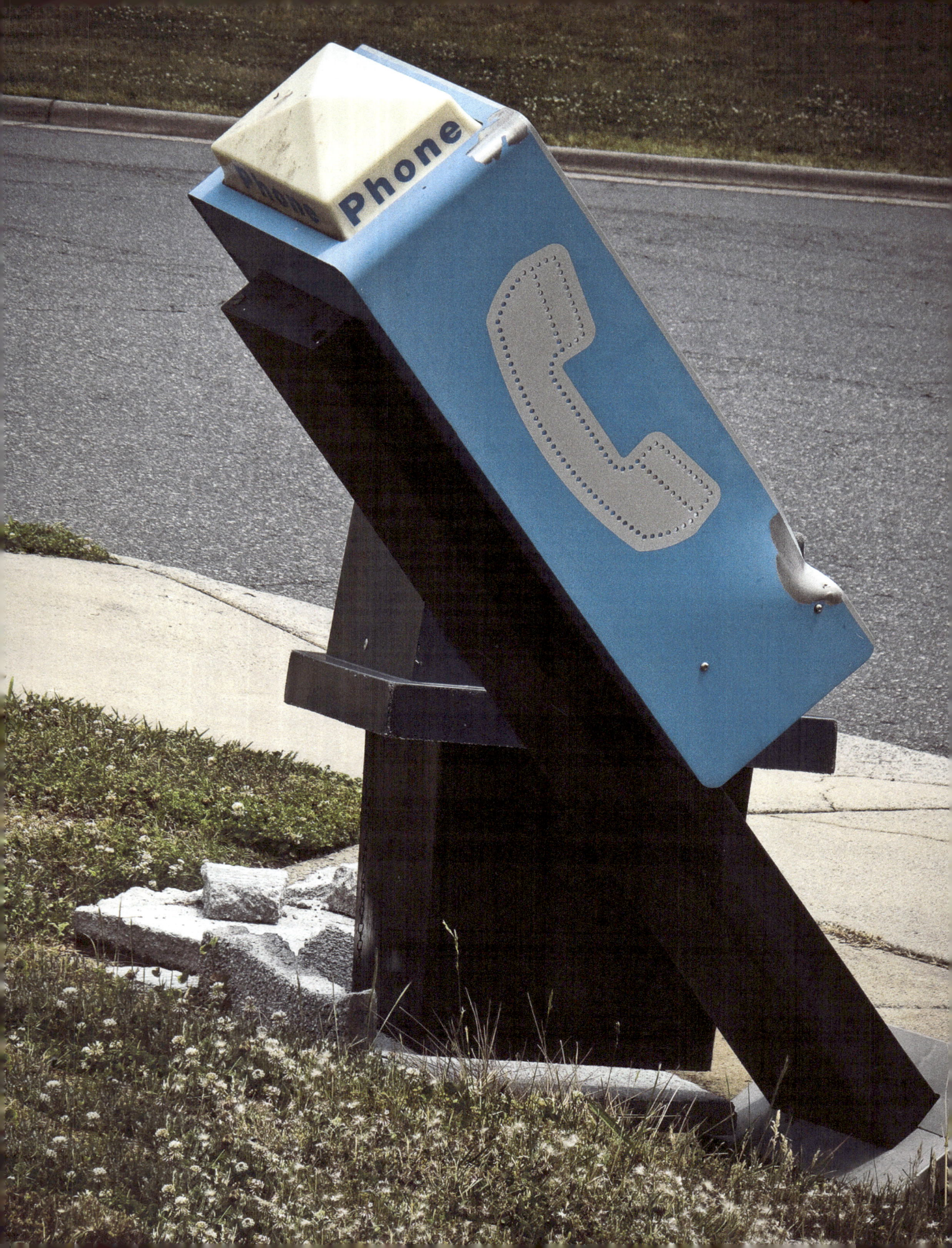

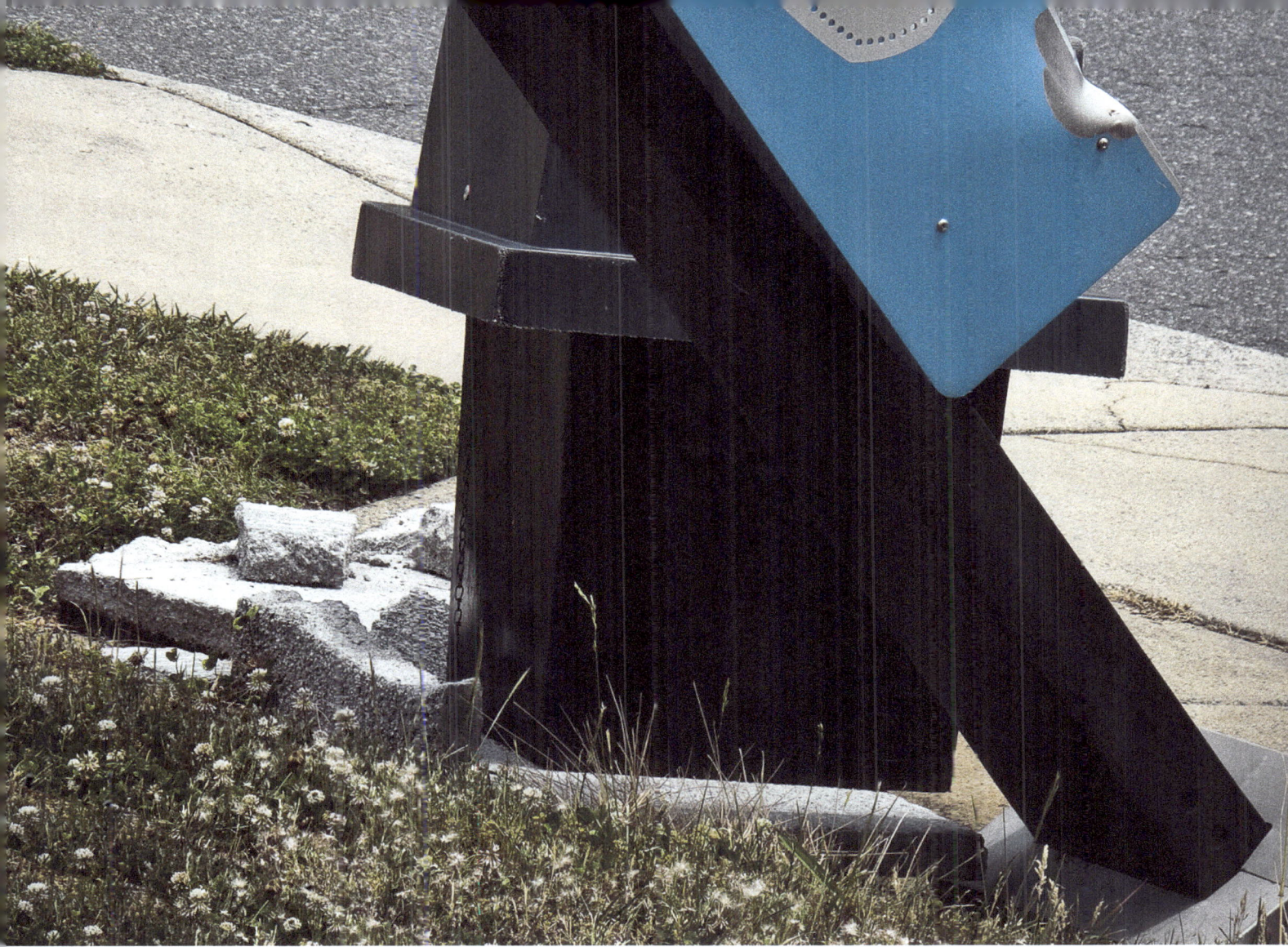

Sign Of Our Times

I had stopped at a rest area on the inter-state, returning from South Carolina, when it caught my eye. There it was. Discarded, leaning over, dented, unattached to its source, (the telephone company.) Right next to it, as if the telephone booth had been placed there, was the epitome of where it was in its stage of life. It was no longer needed, so it rested next to the trash container. We have come a long ways since Alexander Graham Bell. Once needed at nearly every corner, this phone booth and every one like it, really is no longer cost effective, making a profit and therefore ready for the trash heap.

Taken over by cell phones, smart phones, camera phones, the list goes on and on.

The discarded telephone booth and its telephone are a real sign of our times. "We have come a long ways, baby!"

Now, people do not use the phone just for emergencies but for every day, at the moment, conversation. You see them everywhere. In the restaurant, at the bank, at a sporting event, everywhere you turn, someone is using a cell phone.

And what is even more interesting is that the cell phone is being used millions of times each month for "texting," having, it seems, its own language and vocabulary. Kids text each other while they sit in a classroom together or even as they sit in the back seat of a car together. People die because they text and drive.

No, progress is not bad, at all. But, it is not all good as well. One thing is for sure, that telephone booth isn't coming back! (And texting is not going away!)

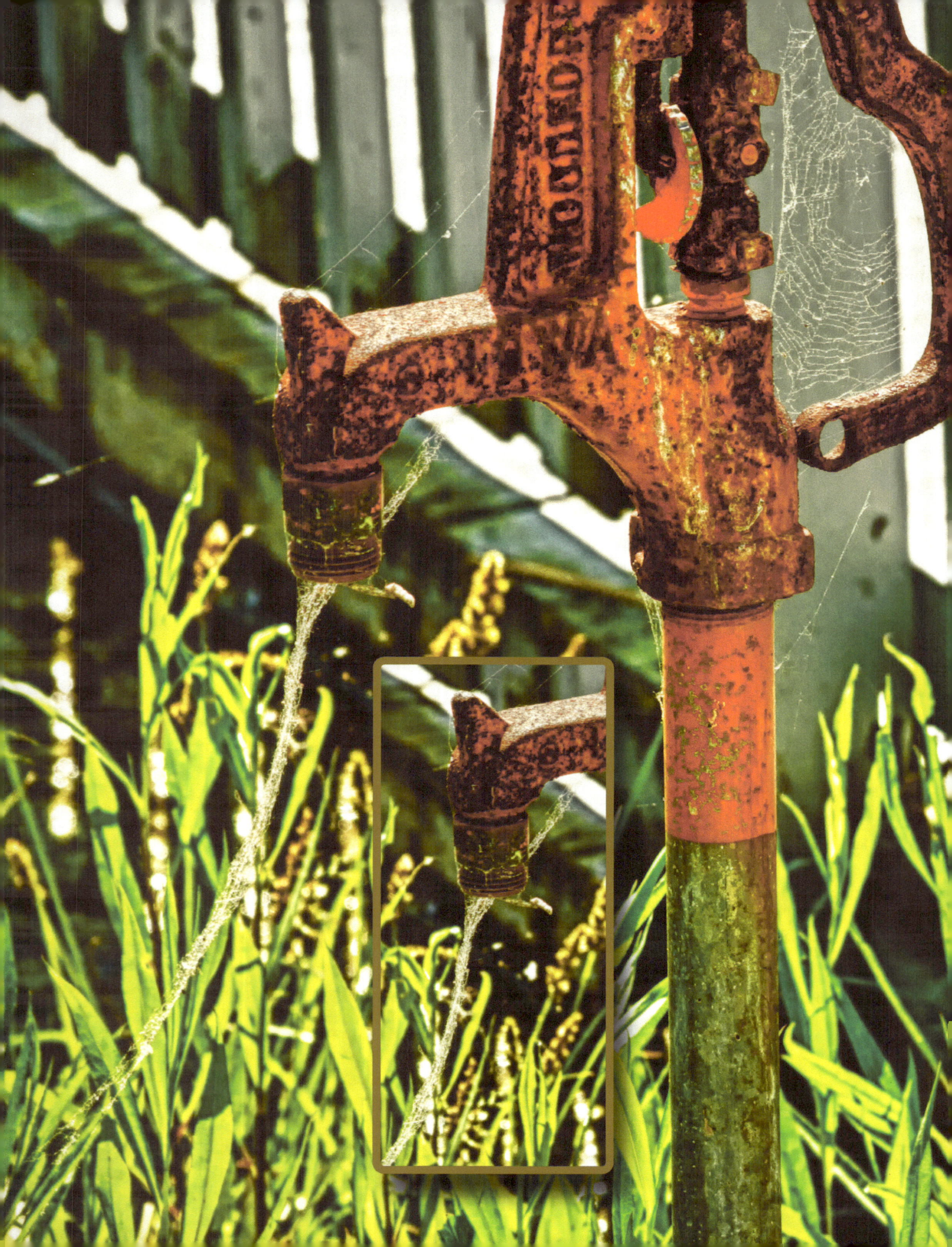

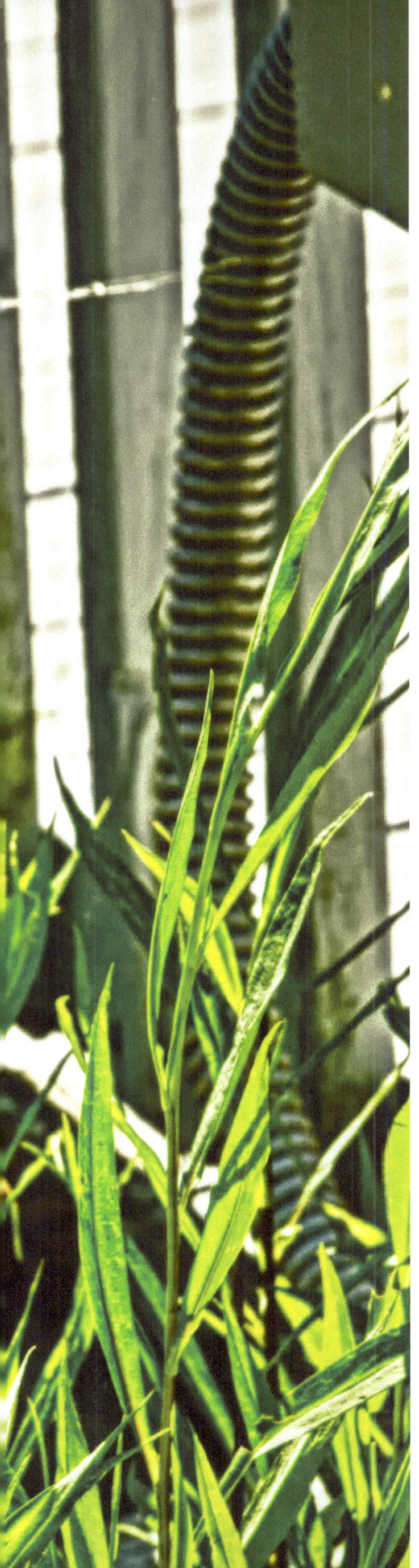

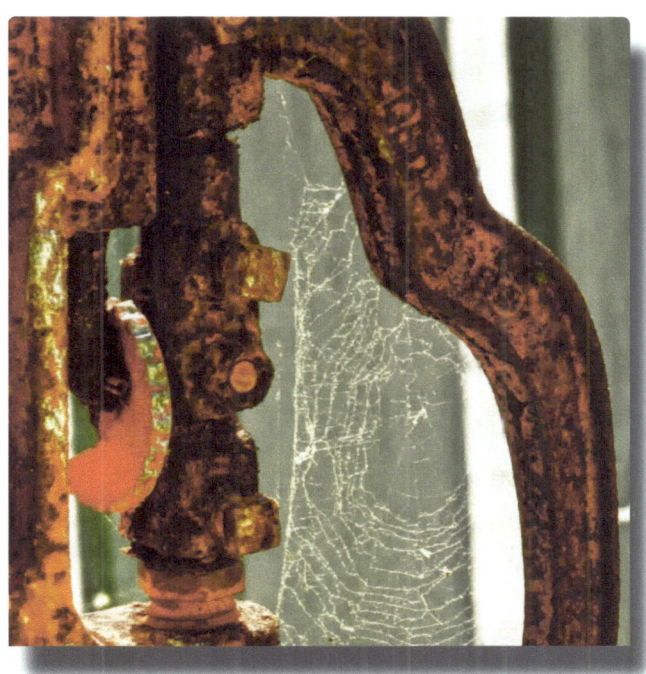

It Won't Pump, If You Do Not Use It...

We were shooting senior pictures at the clients home, down near their pond. As I looked around after taking a shot, I saw it. That orange rusted top, typical pump handle and it looked ready to use.

But then I stopped. Coming from the pump nozzle was a pretty significant spider web. Yes, that speaks volumes, doesn't it? That old pump was either out of commission or not used at all.

These pumps have been around a long time and even though many are still in use, a vast majority are out of commission. Now, we have electrical pumps and other sophisticated pumping operations that this old pump never dreamed of.

As we get older in life, it often seems the same way. We are around, able to operate, but not taken very seriously any longer. The older one gets, it seems the more irrelevant you become to the younger generation. Unlike other cultures, the elderly or "statesperson" is not regarded as having much "worth" in the United States.

I wish I would have paid attention to that so many years ago. I wish I had tried to make a difference to at least one. And yet, as I continue to gain in years, I see that it is possible that the same thing will happen to me. I'll become just like that old pump. Well, I hope I don't have a spiders web or two!!

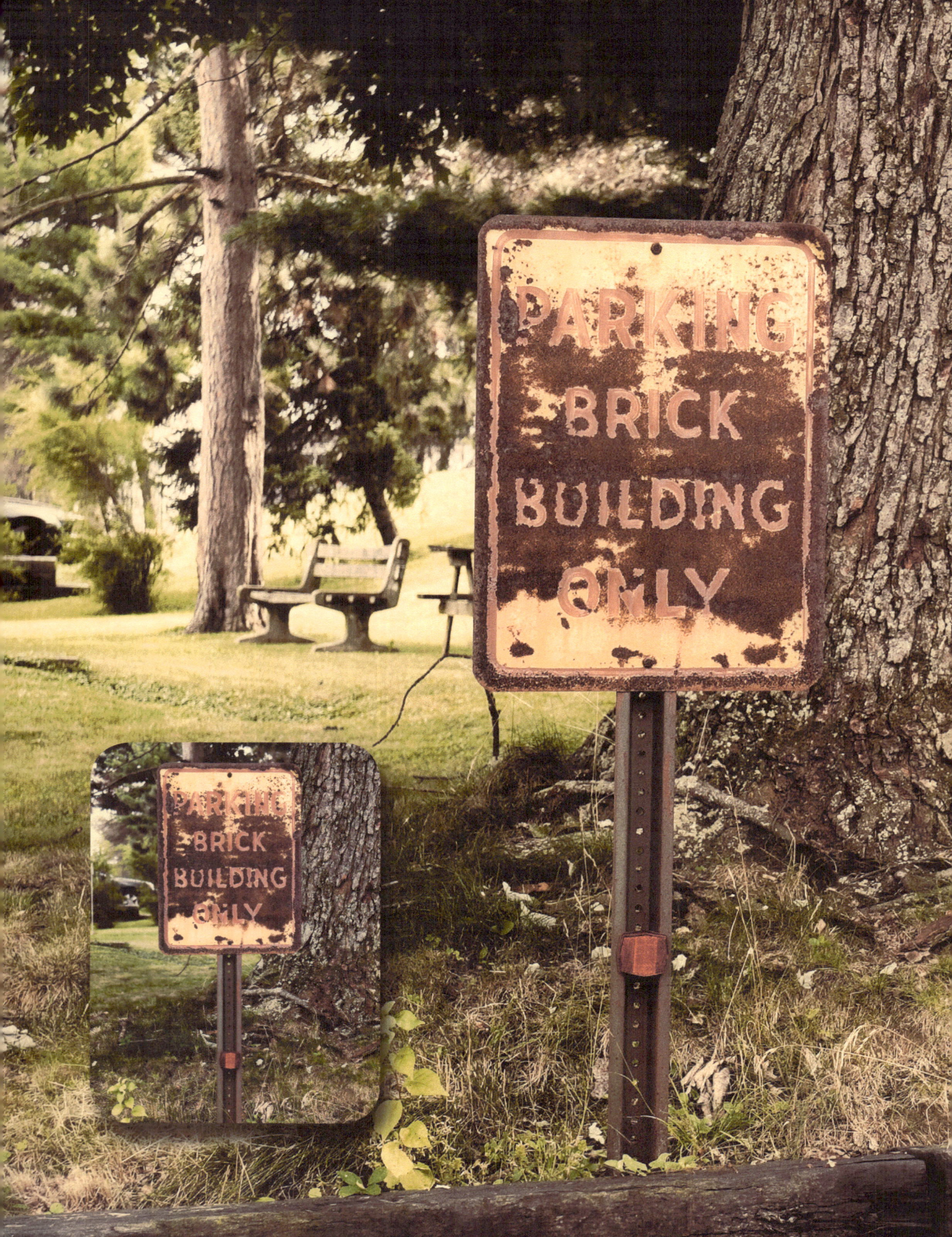

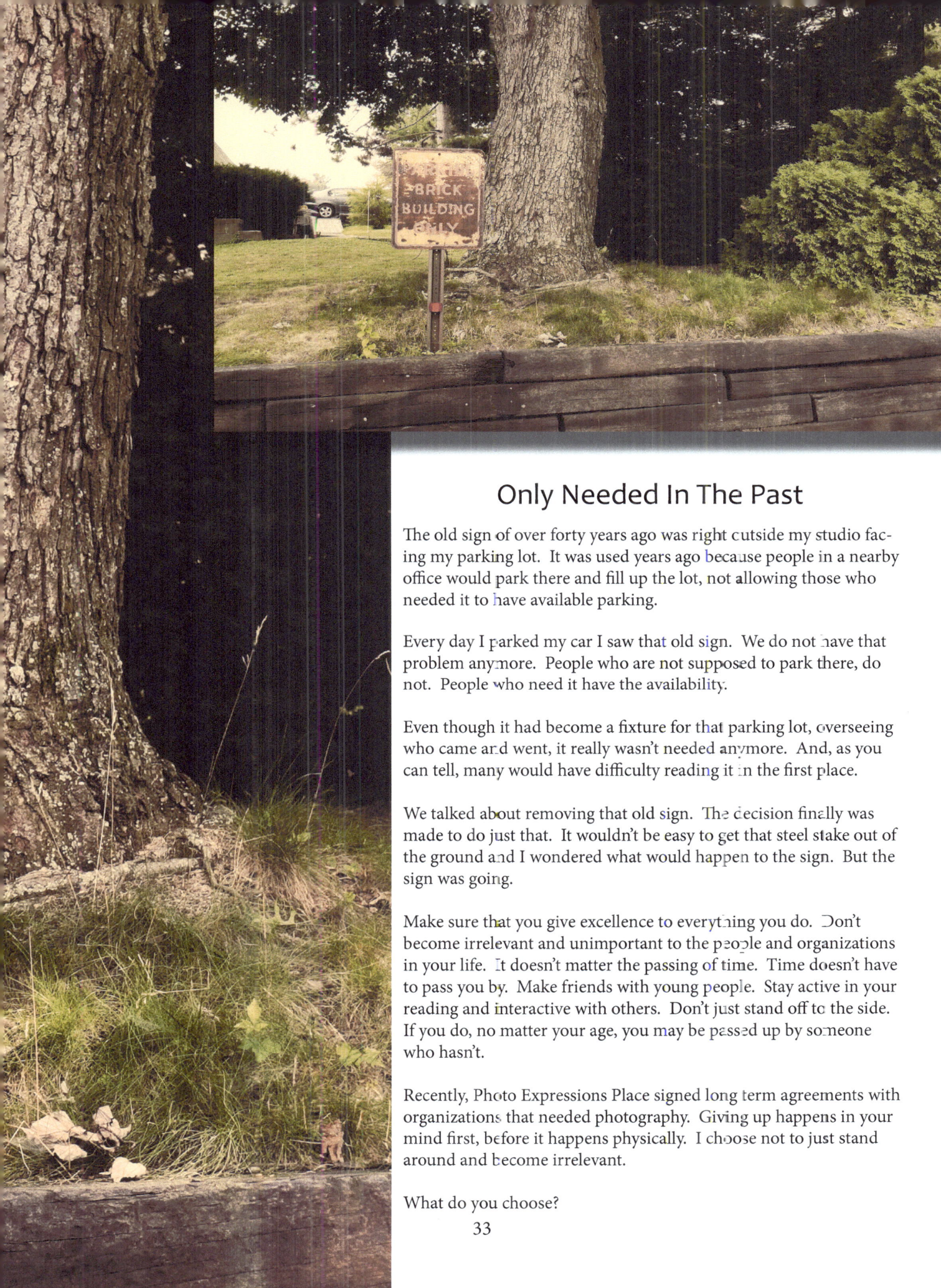

Only Needed In The Past

The old sign of over forty years ago was right outside my studio facing my parking lot. It was used years ago because people in a nearby office would park there and fill up the lot, not allowing those who needed it to have available parking.

Every day I parked my car I saw that old sign. We do not have that problem anymore. People who are not supposed to park there, do not. People who need it have the availability.

Even though it had become a fixture for that parking lot, overseeing who came and went, it really wasn't needed anymore. And, as you can tell, many would have difficulty reading it in the first place.

We talked about removing that old sign. The decision finally was made to do just that. It wouldn't be easy to get that steel stake out of the ground and I wondered what would happen to the sign. But the sign was going.

Make sure that you give excellence to everything you do. Don't become irrelevant and unimportant to the people and organizations in your life. It doesn't matter the passing of time. Time doesn't have to pass you by. Make friends with young people. Stay active in your reading and interactive with others. Don't just stand off to the side. If you do, no matter your age, you may be passed up by someone who hasn't.

Recently, Photo Expressions Place signed long term agreements with organizations that needed photography. Giving up happens in your mind first, before it happens physically. I choose not to just stand around and become irrelevant.

What do you choose?

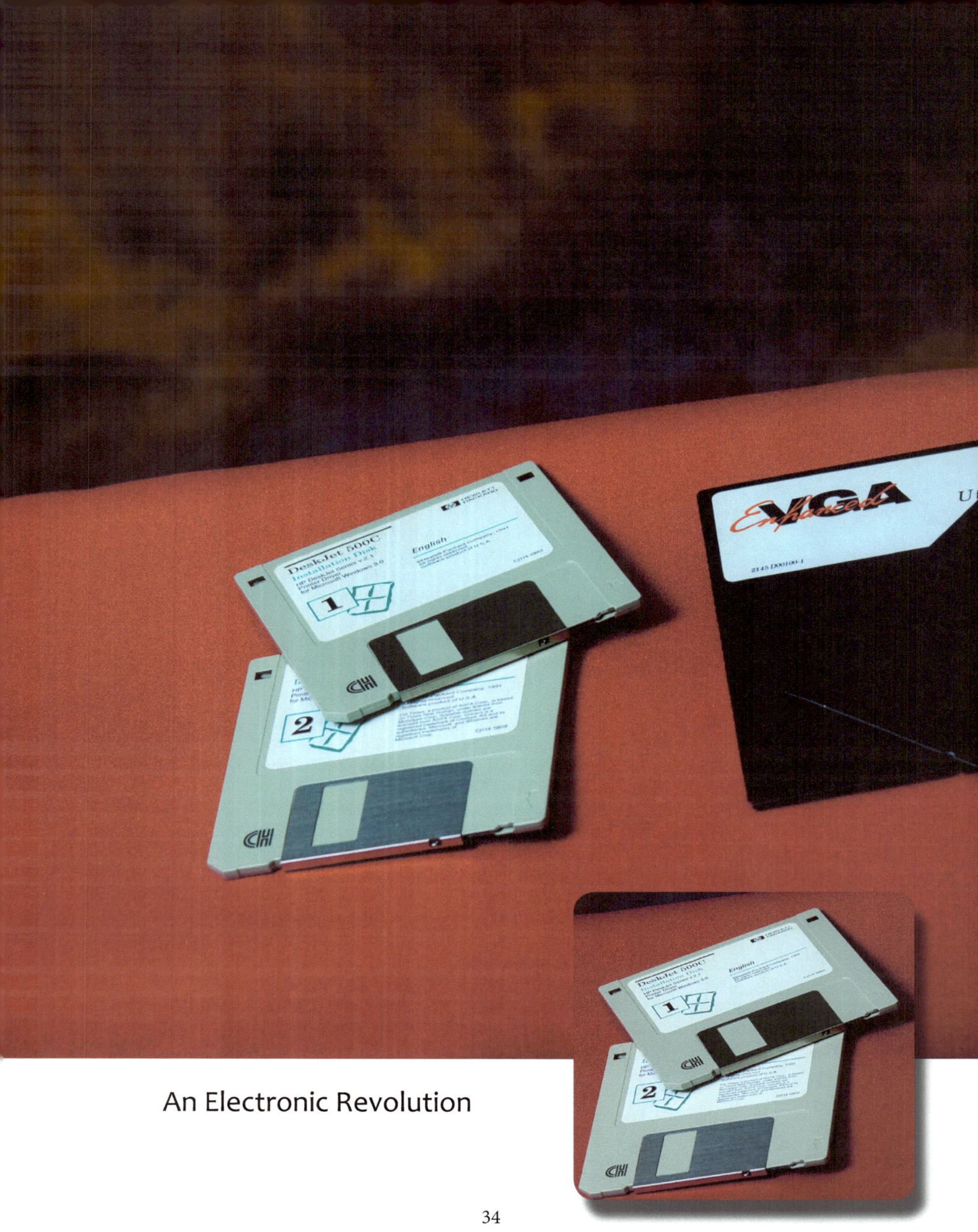

An Electronic Revolution

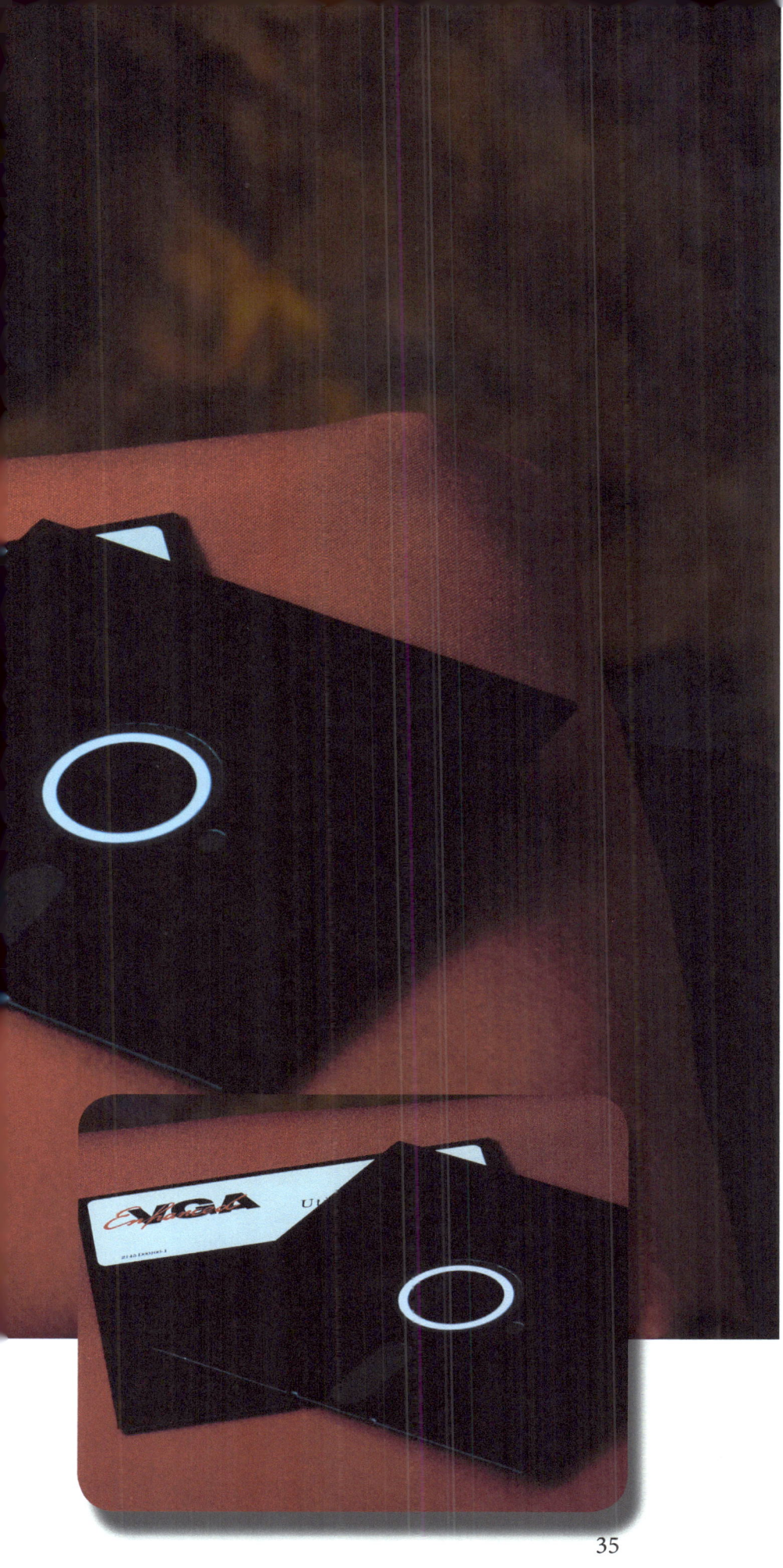

Do you remember those floppy disks and a little later those 3.5" hard disks? Well, we really have come a long ways.

Around thirty years ago I bought my first "consumer" computer. It was a Commodore 64, with 64k of memory. And we thought the world had been turned upside down. Not too long after that, I made a trip to the local computer store, (yes, they actually had those small shops then,) and purchased my first laptop! Well, it really was not a laptop. They called it a portable computer. What a handsome machine it was. All metal casing, a beautiful 6" rectangular color screen and a place for those disks. It was a little bit heavier than today's laptops, weighing in at about 25 pounds! It, too, was a Commodore 64, but I thought I was on top of the world, and way ahead of my time. I used it for several years.

Both floppy and small disks are a thing of the past. Ran across a whole case of the disks recently which belonged to my dad. He had hundreds of his poems on them. Unfortunately, I had no machine to get to them. Fortunately, I have hard copies of them.

However, for twenty-three years I was a pastor, and many of my sermons were put on those disks. They now have been lost (except for the hard copies,) since there is no way to access them.

One lesson we need to learn in the technological age is that whatever mode of memory storage we are using will more than likely be out of date and unusable in the future. Makes you wonder about the CD. DVD, and flash drive.

A lot of wedding couples and high school seniors today buy just the flash drive or CD/DVD from their professional photographer. It looks like, however, more than 90% of the clients are not printing out their digital files. It makes one wonder what they will do if they lose the CD/flash drive or they go the way of the floppy disk and small 3.5" disks and there is no way to access them. How will they recover their memories?

I wonder!

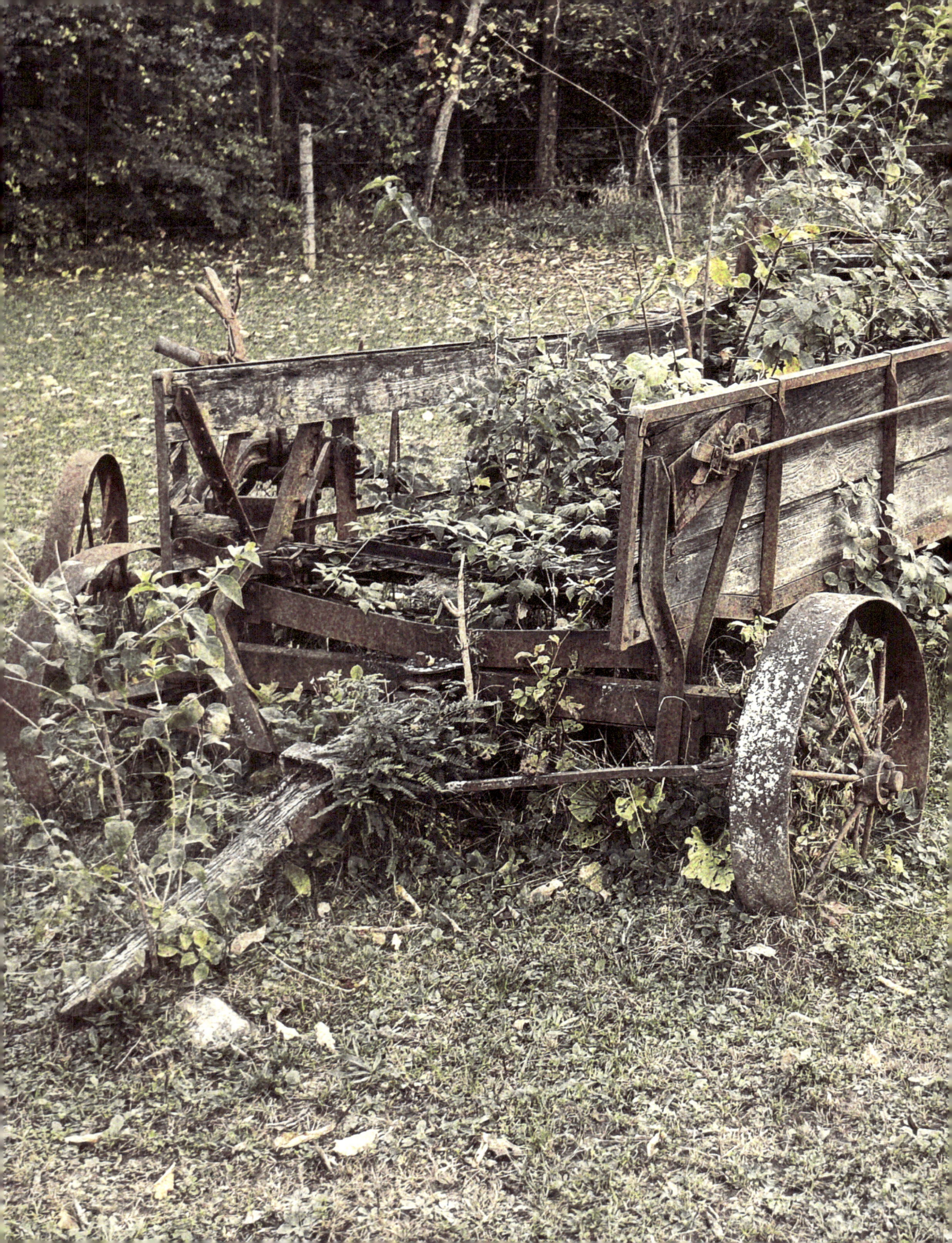

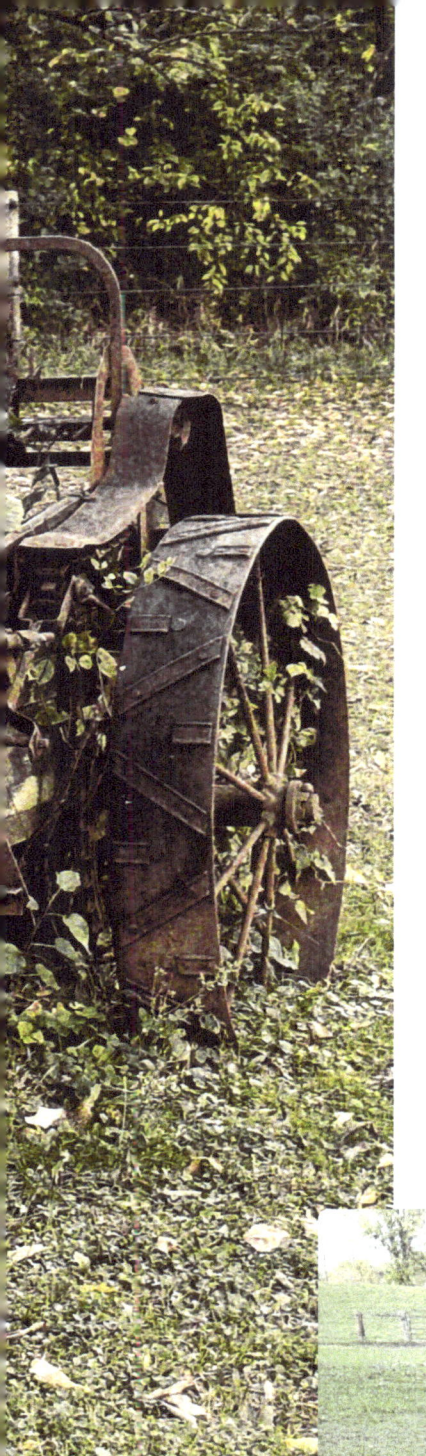

Owner No Longer Wants It!

They say that "beauty is in the eye of the beholder." It certainly is true of this "manure spreader." Once a beautiful piece of farm equipment, though of many years ago, this now rusty, old pile of "junk" is seen by the owner as an eye sore and one that will soon be gone, when it is placed on a large log fire.

However, to this photographer, this is a gorgeous, priceless example of that which has taken on an aura of decadence and though "useless as it is", it is still incredibly beautiful and expressive. No longer does it scoop up and hold manure, no longer is it truly useful, but by "letting it go," it has taken on a beauty of its own, with small trees and weeds growing up through the cracks in the floor and rusty wheels and railings where attractive paint once was placed.

I had been taking a family photo on this farm and looking around. I discovered this manure spreader, "wasting away" out in the field. Disdained by its owner, I, on the other hand saw a beautiful object to be photographed.

Isn't that true in life? Where someone sees an eye sore, another sees an incredible object. As a photographer, I have learned to see things differently, as I began to see things as though I were seeing them through the "view-finder." Have you developed that ability to see things in life differently than you used to? Do you see uniqueness where you once saw something as "plain?"

Whether an object or a person, that really is the challenge.

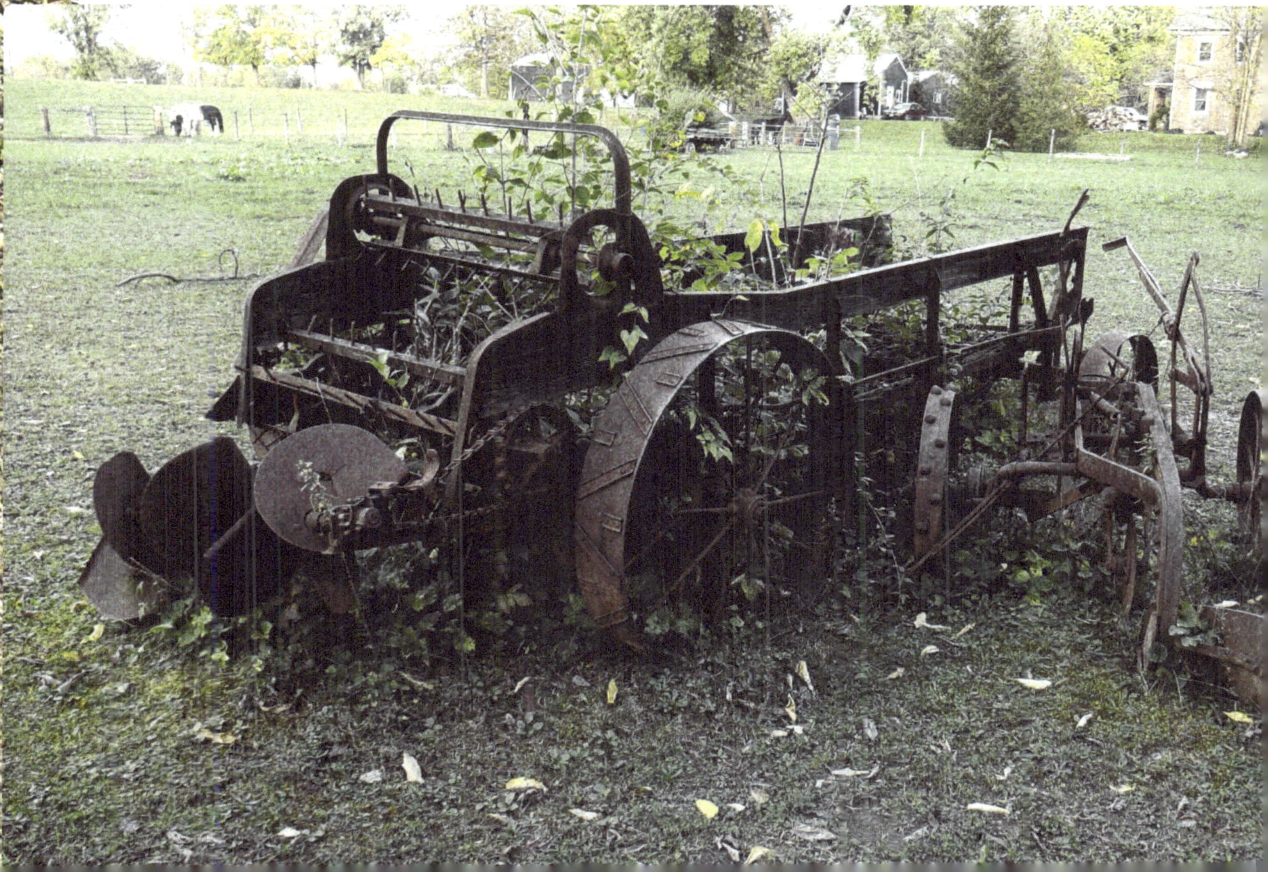

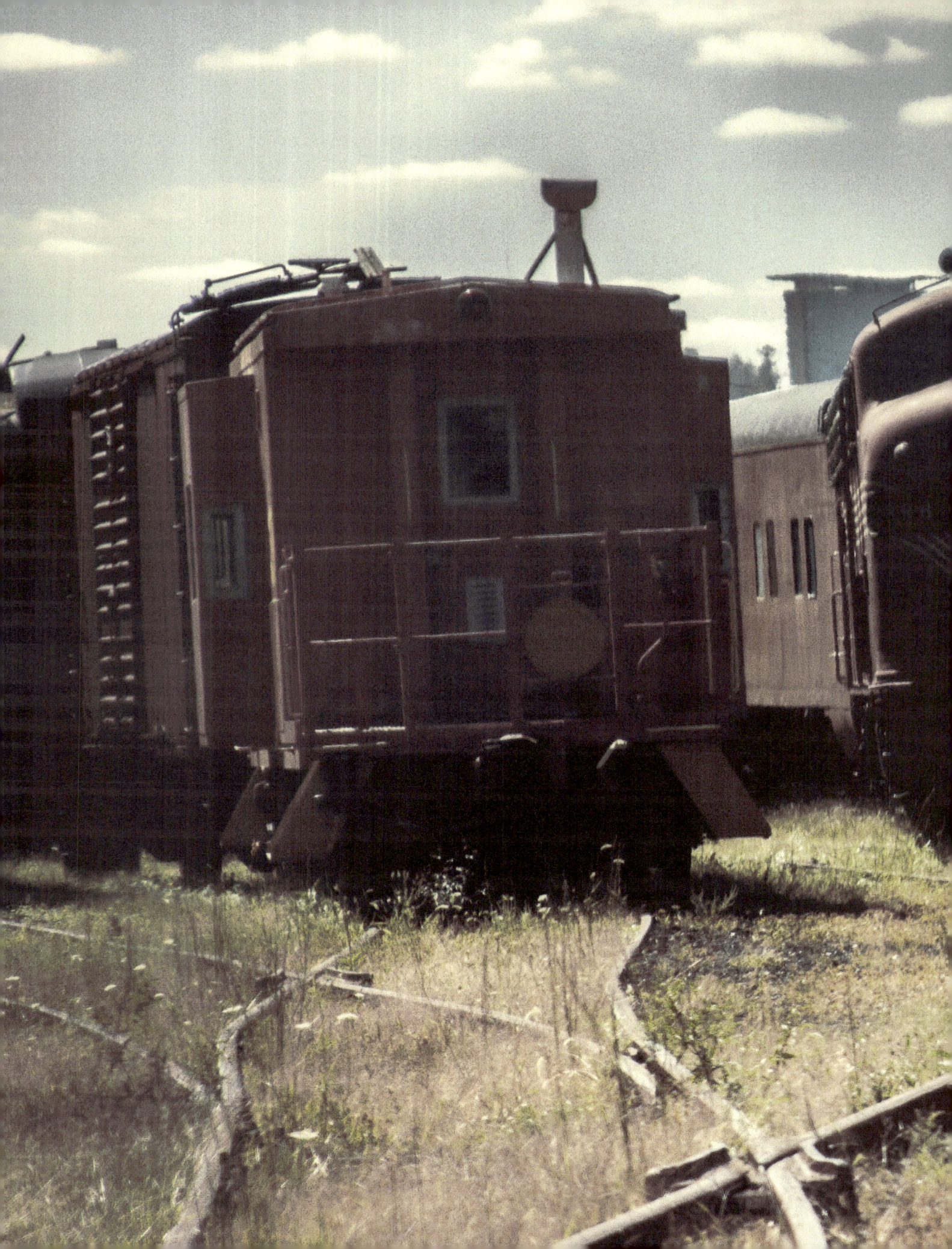

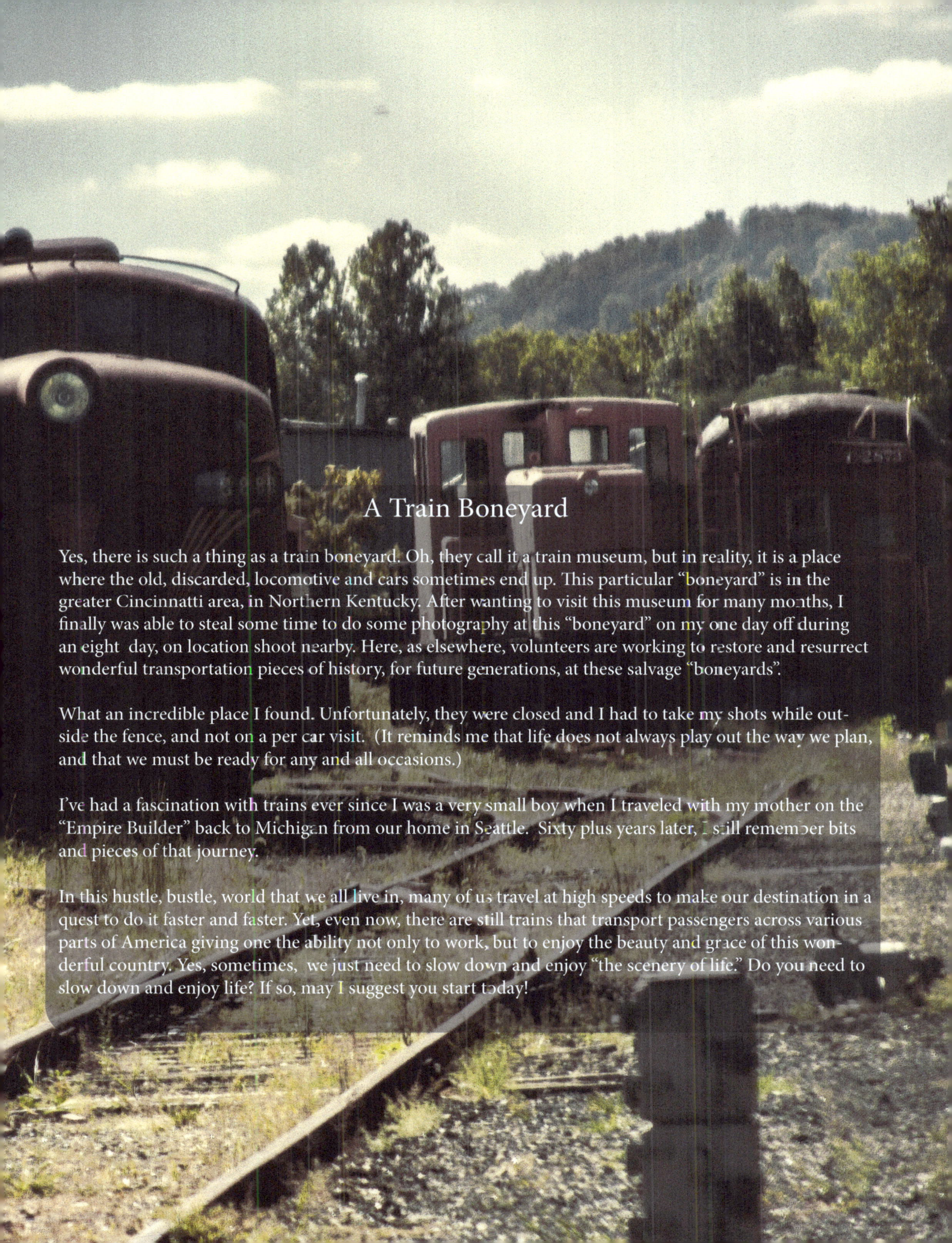

A Train Boneyard

Yes, there is such a thing as a train boneyard. Oh, they call it a train museum, but in reality, it is a place where the old, discarded, locomotive and cars sometimes end up. This particular "boneyard" is in the greater Cincinnatti area, in Northern Kentucky. After wanting to visit this museum for many months, I finally was able to steal some time to do some photography at this "boneyard" on my one day off during an eight day, on location shoot nearby. Here, as elsewhere, volunteers are working to restore and resurrect wonderful transportation pieces of history, for future generations, at these salvage "boneyards".

What an incredible place I found. Unfortunately, they were closed and I had to take my shots while outside the fence, and not on a per car visit. (It reminds me that life does not always play out the way we plan, and that we must be ready for any and all occasions.)

I've had a fascination with trains ever since I was a very small boy when I traveled with my mother on the "Empire Builder" back to Michigan from our home in Seattle. Sixty plus years later, I still remember bits and pieces of that journey.

In this hustle, bustle, world that we all live in, many of us travel at high speeds to make our destination in a quest to do it faster and faster. Yet, even now, there are still trains that transport passengers across various parts of America giving one the ability not only to work, but to enjoy the beauty and grace of this wonderful country. Yes, sometimes, we just need to slow down and enjoy "the scenery of life." Do you need to slow down and enjoy life? If so, may I suggest you start today!

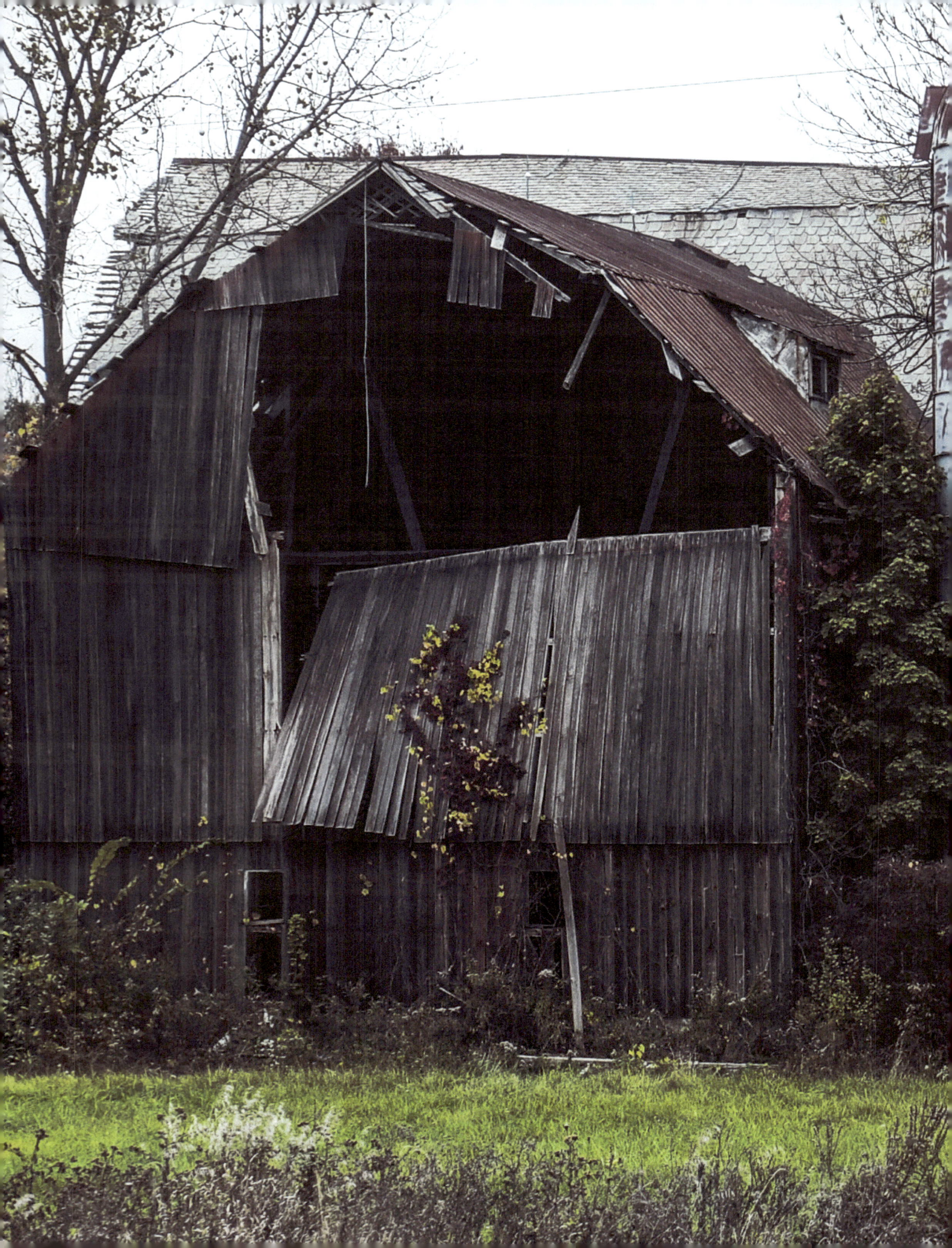

Why?

I have literally driven by this particular barn hundreds of times over the last twenty-seven years. However, it was not until today that it really struck me.

When you become a professional photographer you begin to see things much differently. You begin to look FOR things, and as you view various items your mind reminds you of your latest project or interest. You see life, as though you were looking through the view finder of a camera.

And so it was today. I saw the barn for the very first time, and asked myself, "Why?" Why do we let things decay and fall apart? Why do we allow beautiful edifices and functional facilities to become dilapidated and unavailable for use? Why do we keep them around after they become useless and often become eye-sores for the community around us?

What is it about humans that we really do not seem to care? We let our cars rust, and if they are in an accident and we cannot afford to fix them, we let the dents be dented, and the broken parts be taped up instead of fixed?

Why is it that we leave things out to be destroyed and as a society, we often do not seem to care?

Where is our sensitivity ... and sense of pride, ...and thoughtfulness for others? Why do we do what we do???? I wonder!

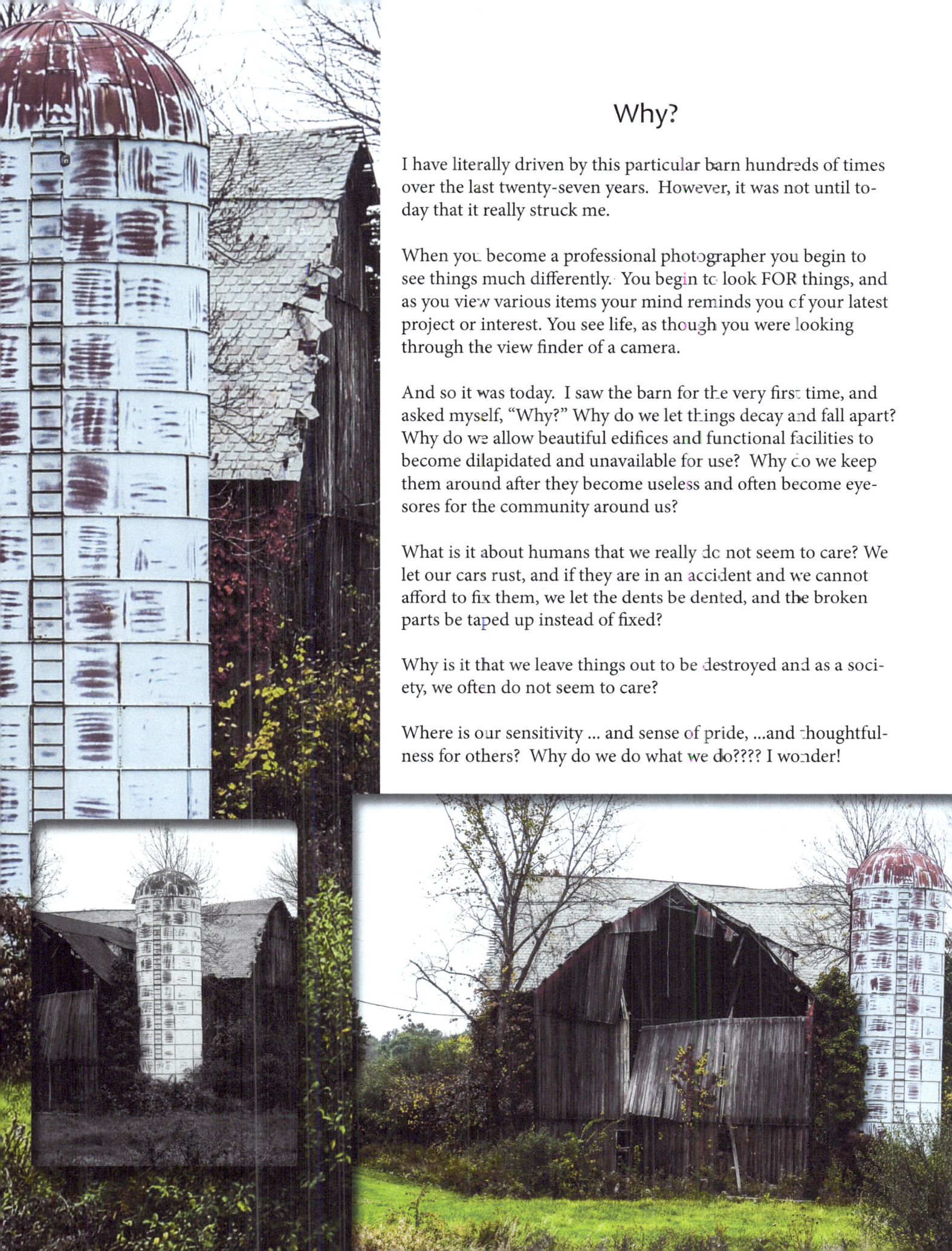

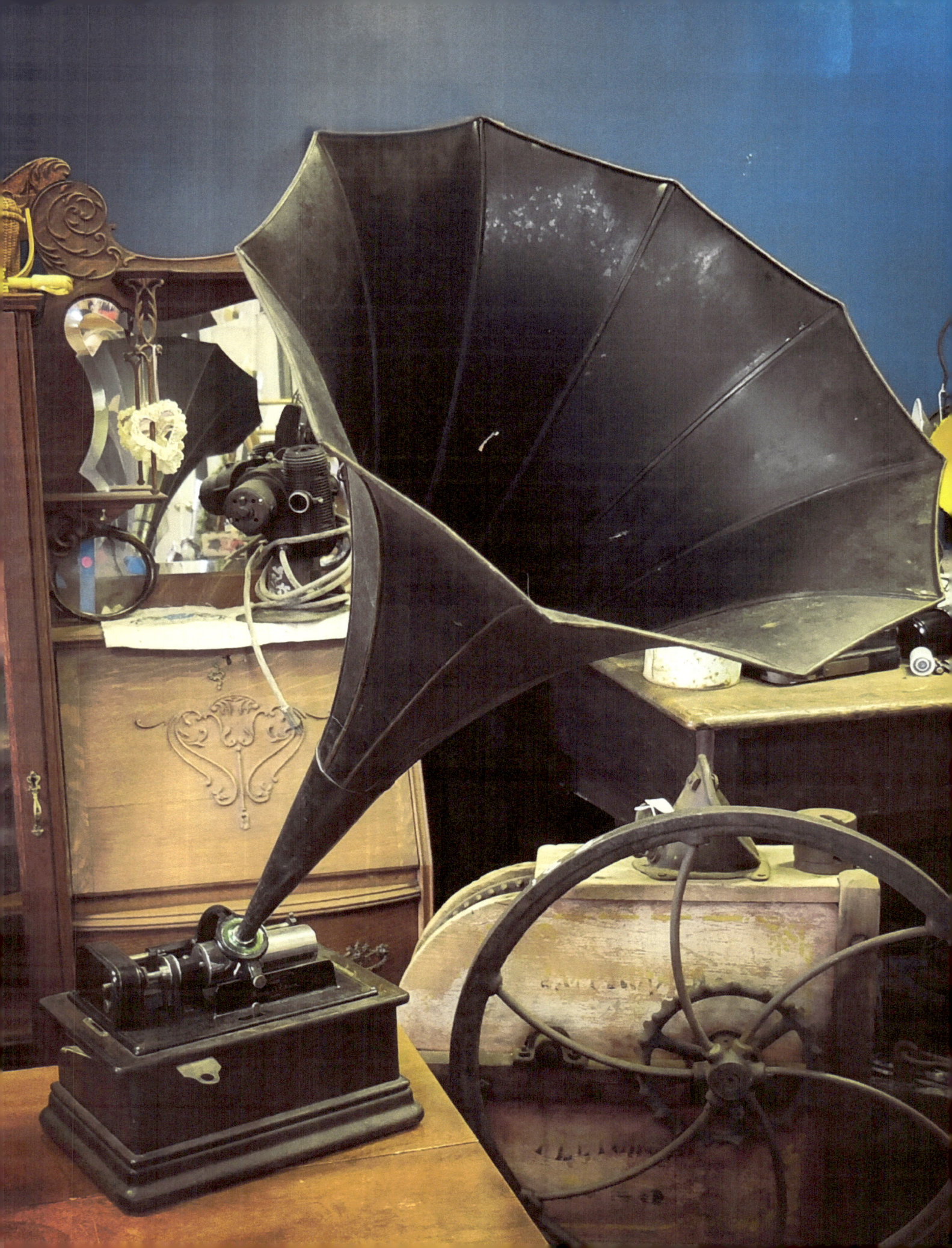

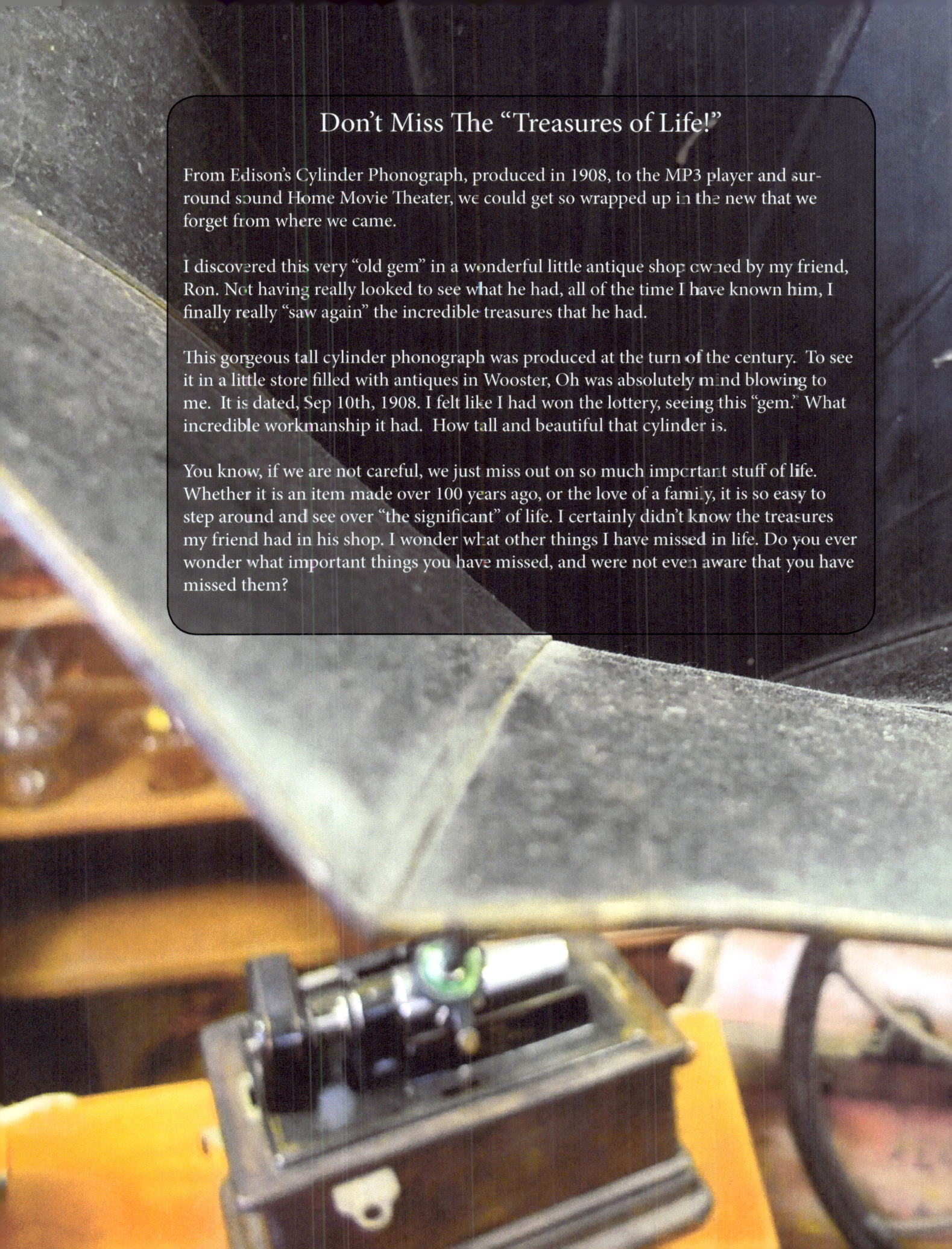

Don't Miss The "Treasures of Life!"

From Edison's Cylinder Phonograph, produced in 1908, to the MP3 player and surround sound Home Movie Theater, we could get so wrapped up in the new that we forget from where we came.

I discovered this very "old gem" in a wonderful little antique shop owned by my friend, Ron. Not having really looked to see what he had, all of the time I have known him, I finally really "saw again" the incredible treasures that he had.

This gorgeous tall cylinder phonograph was produced at the turn of the century. To see it in a little store filled with antiques in Wooster, Oh was absolutely mind blowing to me. It is dated, Sep 10th, 1908. I felt like I had won the lottery, seeing this "gem." What incredible workmanship it had. How tall and beautiful that cylinder is.

You know, if we are not careful, we just miss out on so much important stuff of life. Whether it is an item made over 100 years ago, or the love of a family, it is so easy to step around and see over "the significant" of life. I certainly didn't know the treasures my friend had in his shop. I wonder what other things I have missed in life. Do you ever wonder what important things you have missed, and were not even aware that you have missed them?

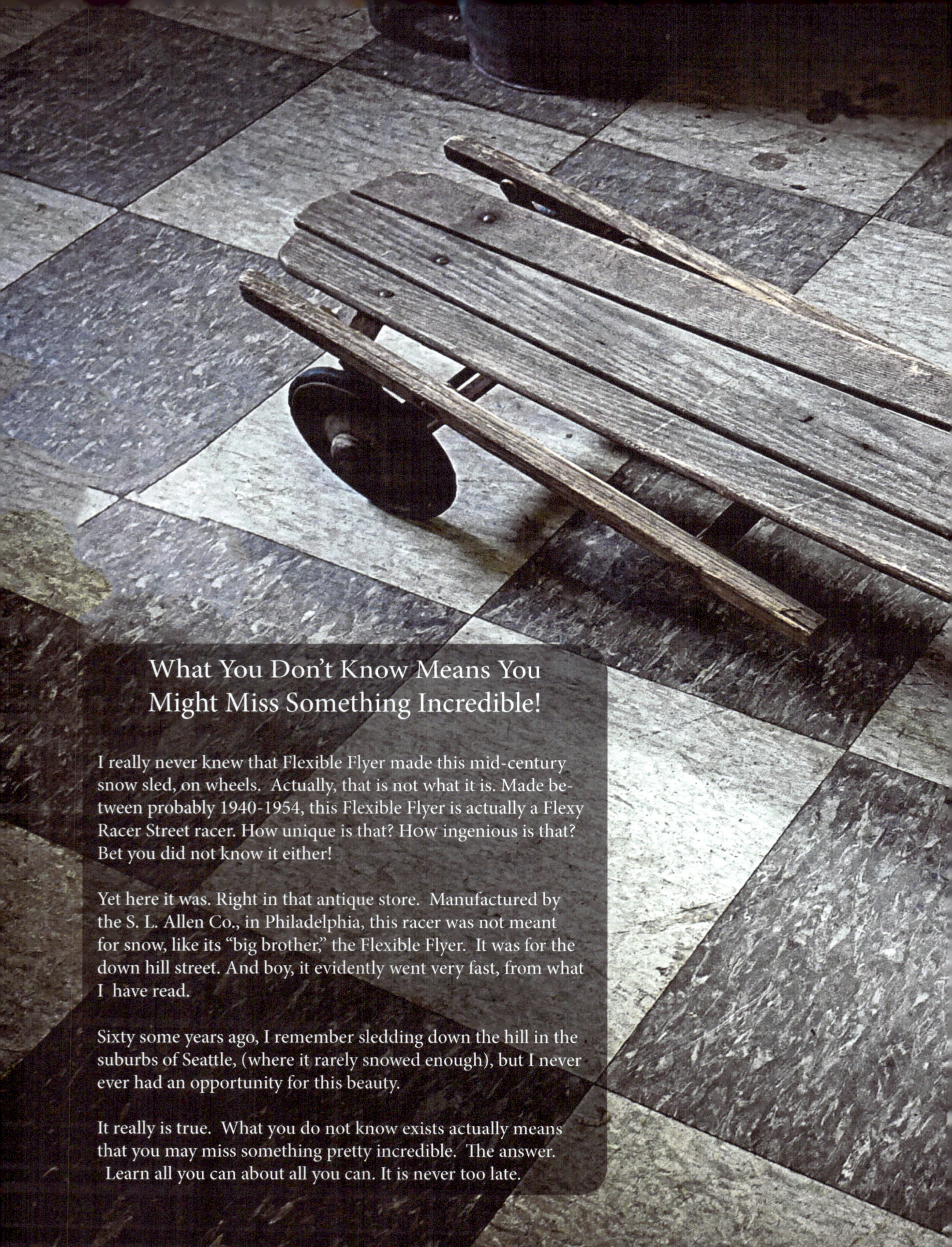

What You Don't Know Means You Might Miss Something Incredible!

I really never knew that Flexible Flyer made this mid-century snow sled, on wheels. Actually, that is not what it is. Made between probably 1940-1954, this Flexible Flyer is actually a Flexy Racer Street racer. How unique is that? How ingenious is that? Bet you did not know it either!

Yet here it was. Right in that antique store. Manufactured by the S. L. Allen Co., in Philadelphia, this racer was not meant for snow, like its "big brother," the Flexible Flyer. It was for the down hill street. And boy, it evidently went very fast, from what I have read.

Sixty some years ago, I remember sledding down the hill in the suburbs of Seattle, (where it rarely snowed enough), but I never ever had an opportunity for this beauty.

It really is true. What you do not know exists actually means that you may miss something pretty incredible. The answer. Learn all you can about all you can. It is never too late.

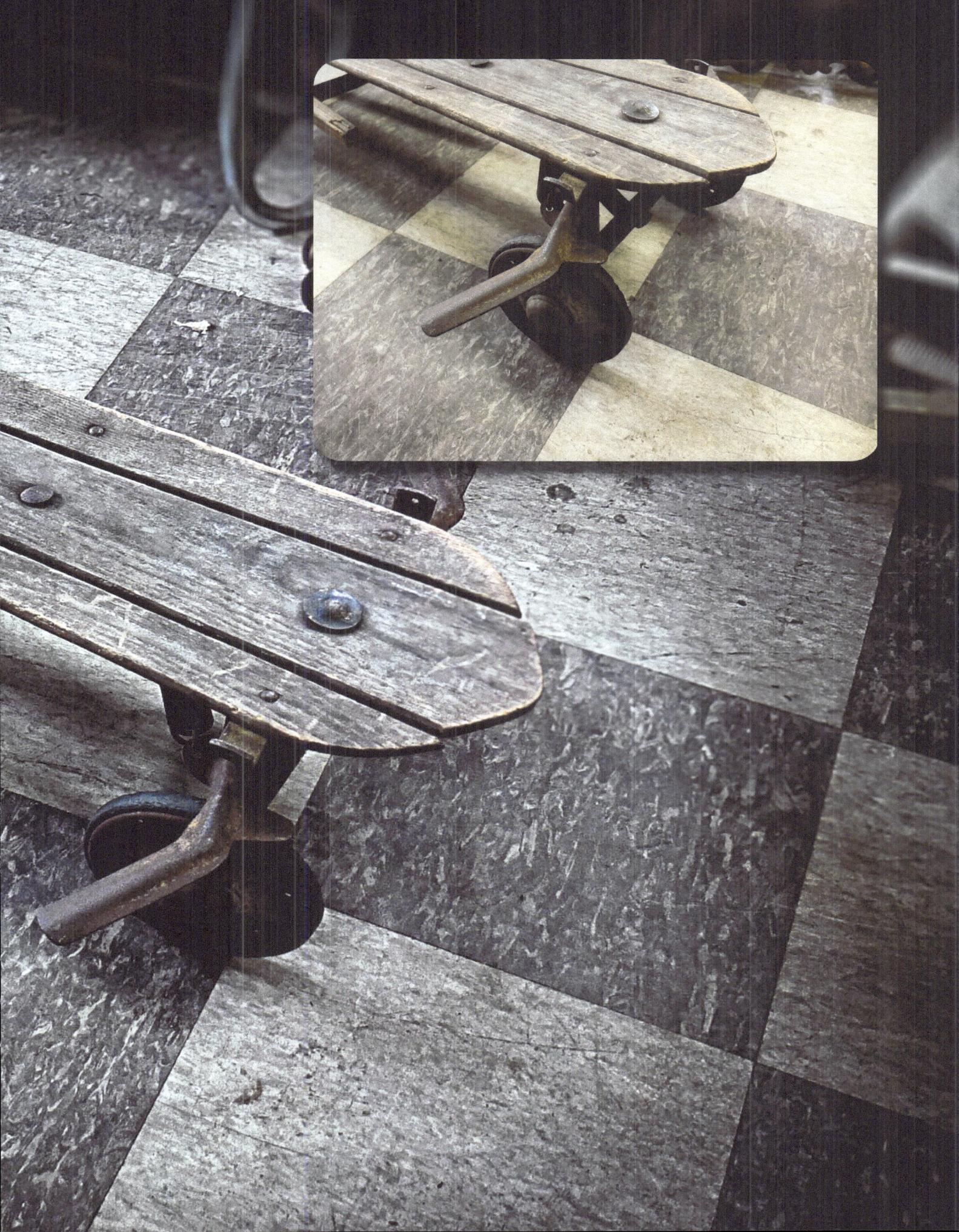

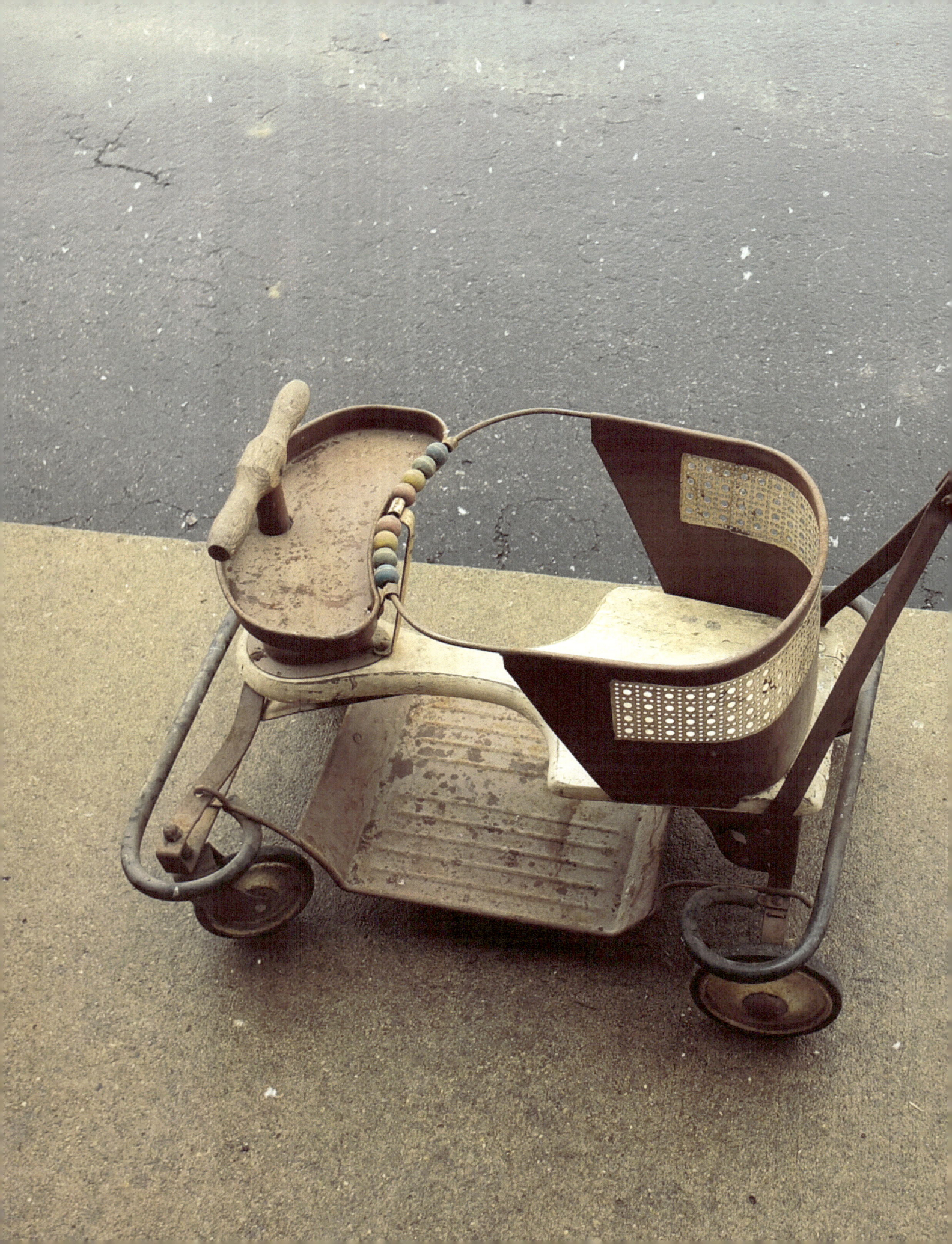

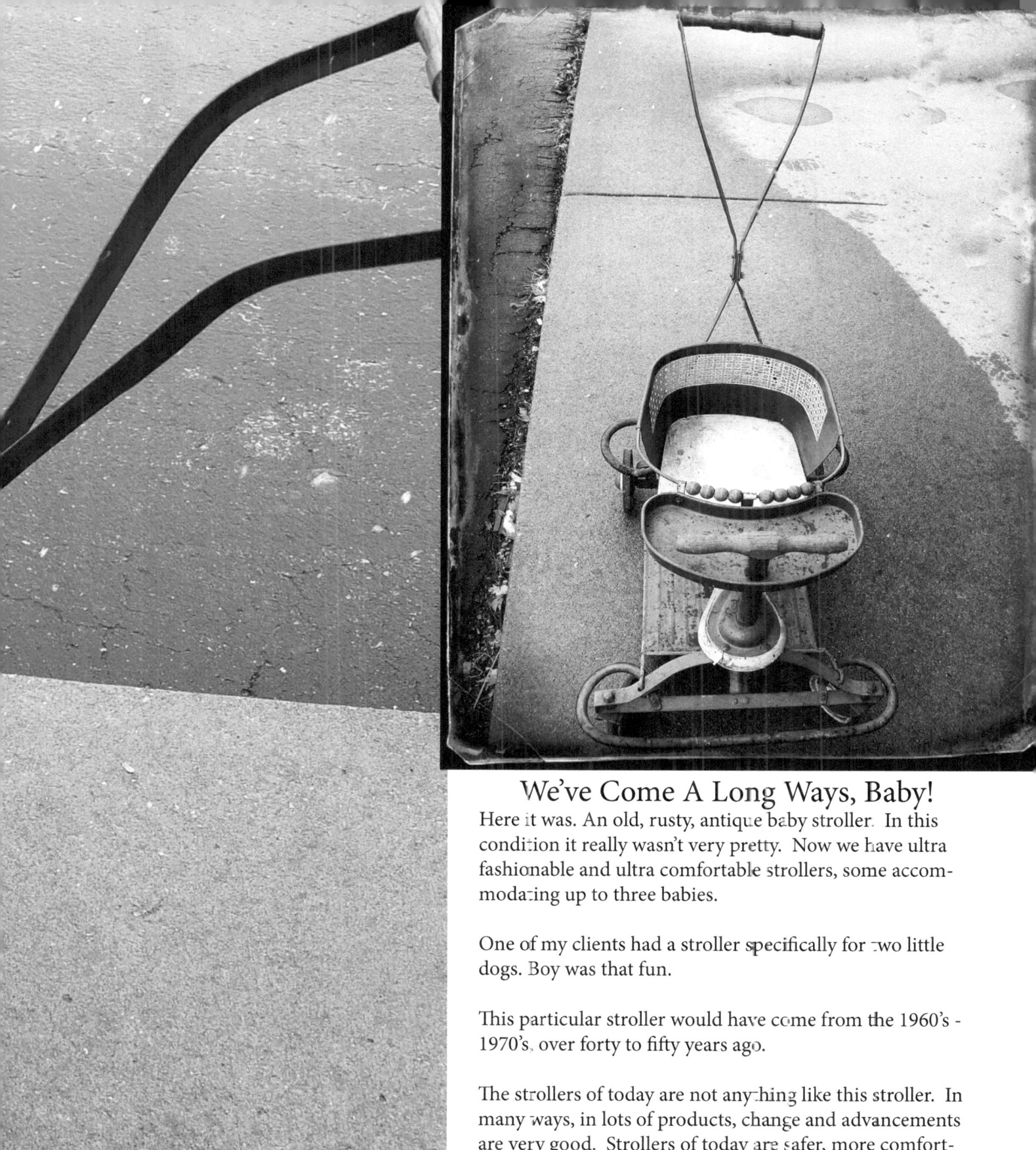

We've Come A Long Ways, Baby!

Here it was. An old, rusty, antique baby stroller. In this condition it really wasn't very pretty. Now we have ultra fashionable and ultra comfortable strollers, some accommodating up to three babies.

One of my clients had a stroller specifically for two little dogs. Boy was that fun.

This particular stroller would have come from the 1960's - 1970's, over forty to fifty years ago.

The strollers of today are not anything like this stroller. In many ways, in lots of products, change and advancements are very good. Strollers of today are safer, more comfortable, more accommodating, and the list goes on. Yet, ...it is easy to say that the years of the past are so much better. As we get older, we often remember the "good old days" with fondness. That really isn't true in a lot of todays products. Advancements are truly good, many times. Think about it!

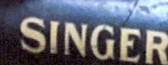

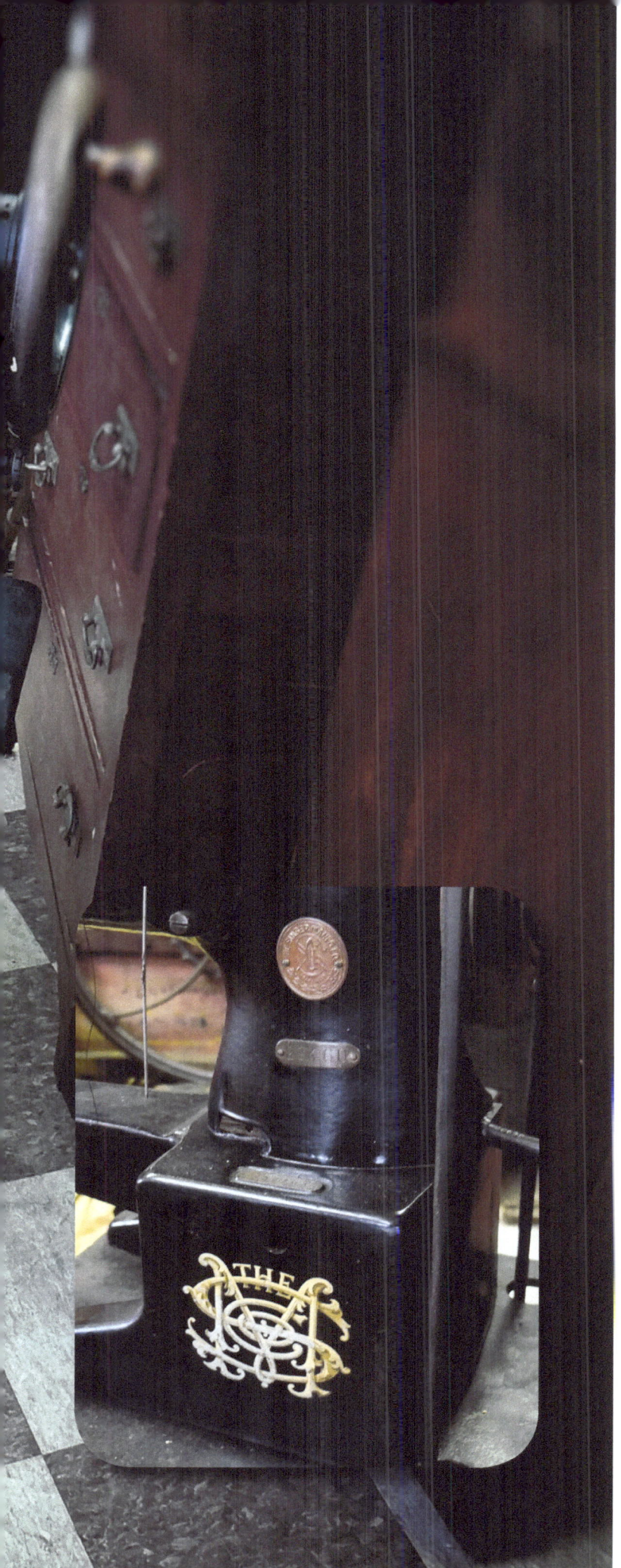

Now, That Was A Sewing Machine...

"Singer" sewing machines have been around since the early 1900's. I dare say that this is no portable model, and I can attest that it is heavy. Gorgeous, but heavy. This treasure was sitting in the antique store waiting for the right person to buy it.

What I didn't realize is that this turn of the century sewing marvel was not made in the United States of America, but in England.

This unit may be over a hundred years old, but it is sturdy, rugged and not easily moved.

Now we walk into the big box stores and buy a portable sewing machine, and carry it out of the store ourselves. Even then, I would bet to say that most households in America, do not even own a sewing machine.

Most people buy their clothes at a big box store or specialty store and if there is hemming to do, they shop it out for a seamstress or seamster to take care of.

I dare say that there are not many (percentage wise) American households that make their own clothes today.

We want "name" brands, the latest fad, the "coolest" clothes, and we want it now! That's a pretty good summation of our society. "Name Brand," "Latest fad," "Cool," and "Impatient."

We have come a long ways from our ancestors. Not all bad, not all good. And in a hundred years you won't find the portable sewing machines still standing like this very old "Singer."

Think about it.

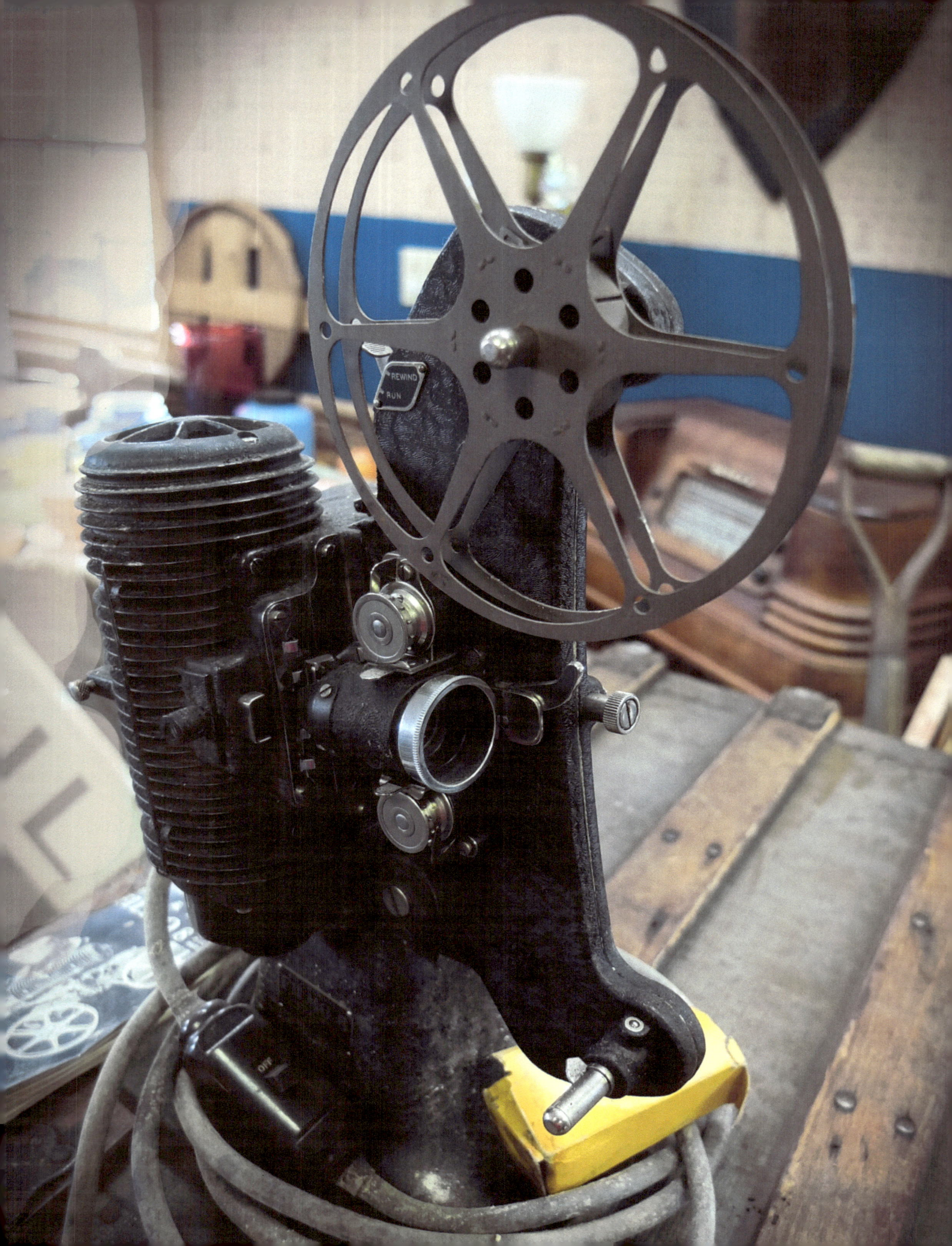

And To Think, Many Of Us Watched Home Movies This Way!

Do you remember those home movies we used to watch on an 8mm film projector?. That was a long time before VHS, dvd's, surround sound home theaters and HDMI. Some of us are old enough to remember. Boy, did we think that the times were special. So, when I saw this old 8mm film projector in an antique store, I knew it had to be photographed.

It would be easy to think of those days as "the good old days." But, in many ways they were not. To many families, it was a struggle, and lots of families had just come out of the Great Depression, which had scarred and shaped them for life.

Even though I have photographed these many images throughout this book, I encourage you to "live in the present." Make every day count! "Pay it forward." Do something good for someone today. Make a real difference in someone's life. Make their day, and yours, a "good day, right here, right now."

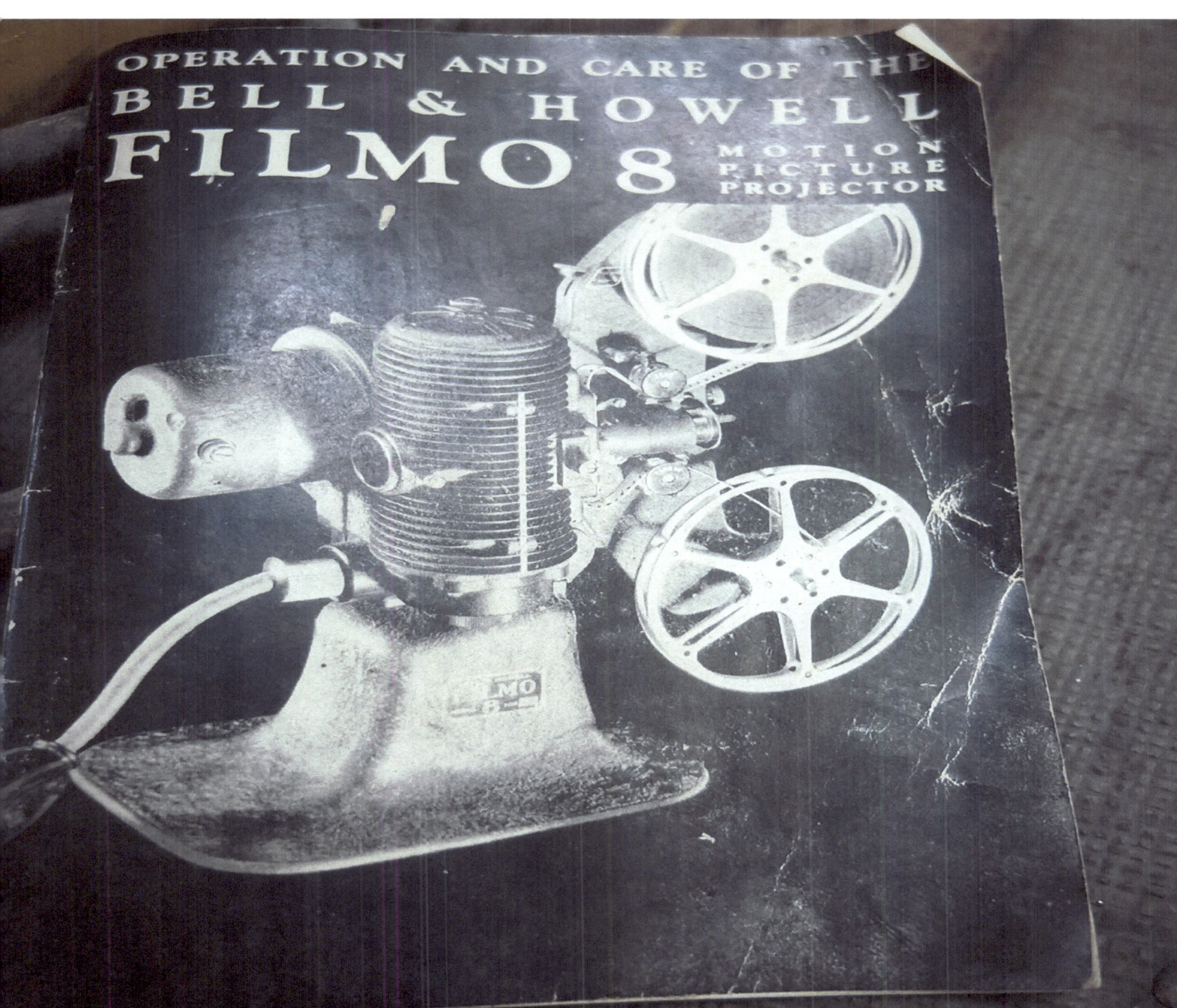

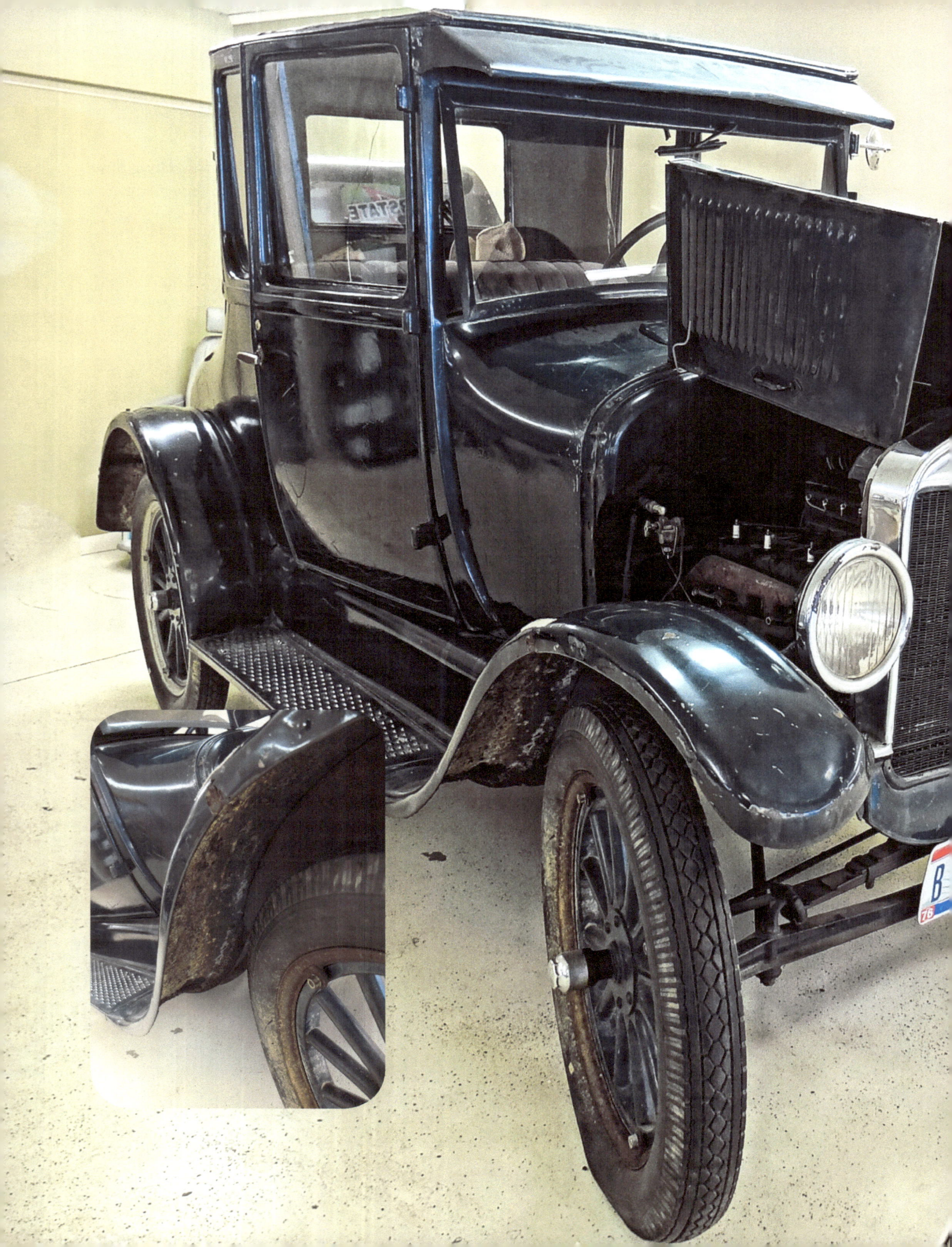

It Isn't Always What It Seems..

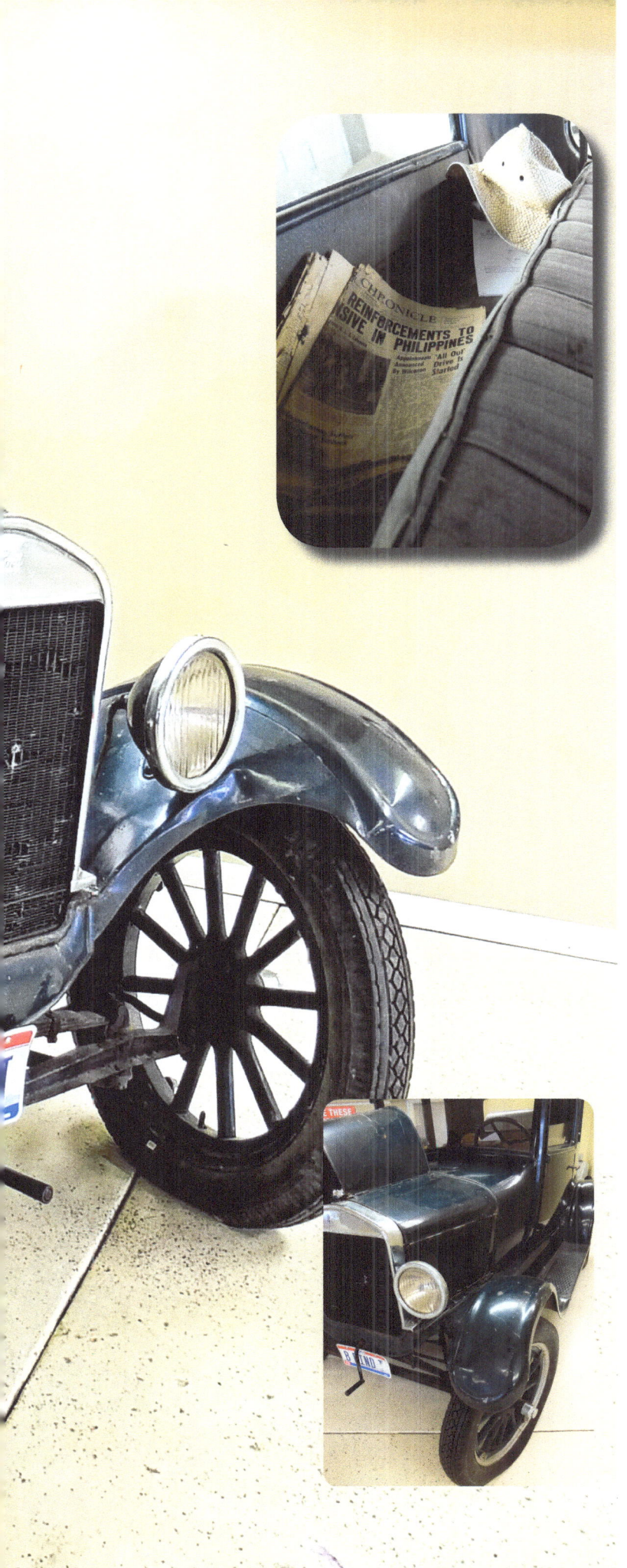

I'm a sucker for antique cars. I love the old car rallys and seeing what individuals have done to restore these old cars to their glory. But then I saw this Model A.

It was in the show/sales area of Jim's Transmission and immediately it caught my attention (and still does.) This car is NOT restored. It has NOT been made a roadster or dragster. There it stood, in all of its prior glory.

When I first became interested in it, this wonderful old Ford, looked like the perfect car for photography shoots, (especially for seniors.) I began to dream and think about how it could be used, how I might be able to purchase it, etc.

But, then, I began to *really* look at it. Sure, it had some really cool things, like that old hat and 1940's newspaper behind the seat. But, this antique car, was far from being in pristine shape. Rust abounded, in areas under the car, in the trunk, around the engine compartment. There is nothing worse than rust to an old car, or any car, for that matter. And then the top was coming apart. This car needed a lot of work. Work I was not prepared for, nor wanted to shell out the thousands of dollars for.

This 1927 "Model A", by Henry Ford, reminded me of a very important lesson, not always learned or remembered. *Before you jump, look again and again. Things are not always as they seem.* Perceived opportunities may, in fact, be disasters ready to happen.

Type A personalities do not always remember that lesson. Sometimes we jump, and then realize the fall is far longer than what we anticipated. It's a hard lesson, but a lesson to be learned. Anyone can fall victim to it.

So, ... the next time you have a great idea or are tempted to act on a perceived wonderful opportunity, just stop, look again, and again, and again. It may not be a gold mine. It may turn out to be a grave.

Epilogue

The preceding pages and their related photographs are just a smattering of the many things that you and I touch and see everyday that is coming passe'. They are no longer used, no longer needed, new advancements and technologies have replaced them.

Frankly, I could have included hundreds more in this book, and in fact, this writing could actually never be completed with the entire myriad of things, buildings, vehicles, that were once available to us but no longer viable.

There are some who are wistful of that, longing for the days long past, collecting and hoarding and enjoying things that are collectible, and yet, sometimes should be thrown in the trash can.

I have taken you on a short journey into the past, by sharing things that are decadent, dying, no longer useful to society. It hopefully has been a journey, not only of photographs, but challenged you to do some thinking, and even change your mind once in a while.

If you are young enough not even to know about some of these things, maybe I have enlightened you. It has been a good past from which we have come. If I have reminded you of something, long forgotten, then I say, "good for you."

But the journey is not over. Find your own things to remember. Tell your own stories. Write down your own memories. Give them to those who follow you. Don't let the past totally die out. Our history is important. We need to learn from it, build upon it, never forget them, but never mourn its passing.

Thanks for accompanying me on this journey.

Paul Donihue
Winter, 2014

About The Author/Photographer

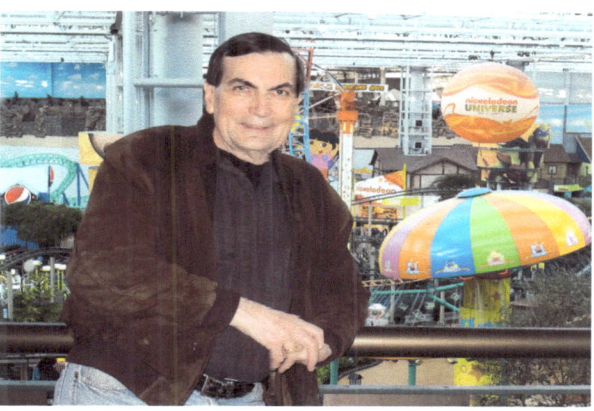

Paul Donihue, a professional photographer, owns Photo Expressions Place LLC, Wooster, Ohio, a full service photography studio / business specializing in event photography, family portraiture, and church directories. After becoming a full time business in the spring of 2012, Photo Expressions Place (PEP) expanded its church directory division regionally into three states in less than seven months.

A businessman, (co-owner of a national business solutions company , Business Success Enterprises, specializing in helping small and medium sized companies grow); and author of two business books, "11 Ways To Kill Your Business," and "Love Your Job;" Paul is also a public speaker, seminar leader and author of the complete business development turn-key system for professional photographers, "Ready, Set, Connect! Drive Your Revenue With Church Directory Photography." An ordained clergy, Paul successfully pastored churches in Michigan, Pennsylvania and Ohio for a total of twenty three years.

Paul is a member of Professional Photographers of America (PPA,) The Akron (Ohio) Association of Professional Photographers, International Freelance Photographers Association (IFPA), US Press Corps. Org, Photo Marketing Association (PMA); Professional School Photographers Association (PSPA); Sports Photographers Association of America (SPAA); Digital Image Marketing Association (DIMA); and Association of Imaging Executives (AIE).

Paul, lives in Wooster, Ohio, with his wife, Patricia of forty-four years, as well as their Puggles dog, Snickers.

You may reach him at pdonihue@photoexpressionsplace.com.

1. LinkedIN: http://www.linkedin.com/pdonihue
2. Facebook: http://www.facebook.com/photoexpressionsplace
3. Facebook: http://www.facebook.com/MakingRainWithPhotography (a Facebook page for professional photographers)
4. http://www.photoexpressionsplace.com
5. http://www.todaysbizsolutions.com

www.ingramcontent.com/pod-product-compliance
Lightning Source LLC
Chambersburg PA
CBHW050801180526
45159CB00004B/1505

* 9 7 8 0 9 7 9 8 4 6 3 3 5 *